The
United
Nations

THE OLIVER WENDELL HOLMES LECTURES
delivered at the Harvard Law School
in April 1961 under a fund established
out of a legacy at the Law School from
the late Justice Holmes.

THE OLIVER WENDELL HOLMES LECTURES · 1961

The United Nations

Constitutional Developments, Growth, and Possibilities

BENJAMIN V. COHEN

Harvard University Press
Cambridge, Massachusetts
1 9 6 1

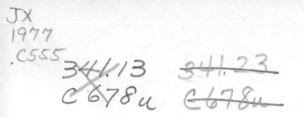

Distributed in Great Britain by the Oxford University Press, London

Library of Congress Catalog Number 61–16691

Printed in the United States of America

Foreword

These Holmes lectures were delivered on April 17, 18 and 19, 1961, the week of the abortive Cuban invasion. Months earlier I chose the United Nations as the subject of the lectures because I felt that amid professions of faith in the Charter there has been in recent years a perceptible decline in the use of the United Nations for the peaceful settlement or containment of international conflicts. The Great Powers seem content to use the United Nations as a diplomatic weapon in the Cold War, avoiding its use as an instrument to aid in the finding of peaceful solutions or accommodations. There are, to be sure, reasons accounting for these adverse developments—ideological differences between the East and the West and marked contrasts in social and economic conditions between the North and the South. But if the growing tendency of the Great Powers to downgrade the United Nations is not arrested and reversed, we may lose our last best hope of peace on earth.

A consensus among the Great Powers on new approaches to peace through the United Nations is urgently needed. It is my hope that these lectures may stimulate thinking on how such consensus is to be achieved.

May 1, 1961   Benjamin V. Cohen.

Contents

The
United
Nations

Chapter 1

Charter Power:
The Competence of
United Nations Organs
Under the Charter

JUSTICE HOLMES's work did not carry him in any marked degree into the field of international law and politics. Yet much of his life was given to interpreting and applying the American Constitution to meet the needs of the peoples of the constituent states in a changing and growing America. Moreover, there is much in Justice Holmes's contribution to our own constitutional history and development that, by way of precedent and analogy, can illuminate, and has illuminated, the possibilities of growth and development under the Charter of the United Nations. It is not inappropriate, therefore, for me to take, as the subject of the Holmes lectures this year,—The United Nations: Constitutional Developments, Growth, and Possibilities.

There are, to be sure, basic differences between the American Constitution and the Charter of the United Nations. Our American Constitution established a federal government with limited but significant powers over the citizens of the several states as well as over the states themselves. It is more difficult briefly to describe the nature of the international organization established by the Charter of the United Nations. The Security Council has limited authority to determine the legal rights and duties of states. But in most situations, for practical as well as legal reasons, the action of the Security Council, like that of the General Assembly, is essentially recommendatory and is not, generally speaking, legally mandatory. We might say, therefore, that the Charter of the United Nations established an organization through which sovereign states can voluntarily co-operate, with a view to harmonizing their ideas and uniting their strength to achieve common ends. While the American Constitution established a government with organs endowed with power to act, the United Nations' Charter established an instrument for international co-operation. But both created an organism capable of life and growth; the life and growth in each case depending not simply on the written injunctions of the founding fathers but on the vision and wisdom of succeeding generations.

The Charter of the United Nations is a treaty, but not an ordinary treaty. The Member States which subscribe to the Charter not only commit themselves to act in pursuance of the purposes and in conformity with the principles of the Charter, but authorize the Organization to ensure that non-Member as well as Member States act in accordance with the principles of the Charter, so far as may be necessary for the maintenance of international peace and security. The Charter looks toward, if it does not establish, a worldwide community of nations dedicated to the purposes and principles of the Charter.

It is not necessary to recite at length the purposes and principles of the Charter, as enumerated in Articles 1 and 2 and as embellished in the Preamble. Without desiring to provoke a discussion of "preferred" rights or purposes or principles under the Charter, it might be said that the primary purpose of the Charter is that stated in Paragraph 1 of Article 1, "to maintain international peace and security." All of the other purposes are designed to strengthen and safeguard the primary purpose of maintaining peace among nations. The basic principles that states must observe and respect in order to pursue and attain the primary purpose of the Charter are those found in Article 2, paragraphs 3 and 4. Paragraph 3 provides that all members shall settle their international disputes by peaceful means in such manner that international peace and security, and justice, are not endangered. Paragraph 4 provides that all members shall refrain in their international relations from the threat or use of force against the territorial integrity or political independence of any state or in any other manner inconsistent with the purposes of the United Nations. Those two paragraphs in my view constitute the basic law of the Charter.

The basic law of the Charter sets forth the principles by which nations must live if mankind is to survive in this nuclear age. It has been suggested that the Charter was in a sense obsolete when it was adopted because it was framed before the draftsmen knew of atomic energy and nuclear power.[1] Such statements belittle the broad purposes and principles of the Charter and the potentialities for life and growth contained within its flexible provisions. The maintenance of peace is the primary purpose of the Charter. That certainly must be the primary purpose of any international organization dedicated to the survival of man in this nuclear age. The Charter requires all states to agree to refrain from the use of force or threat of force as an instrument of national or ideological policy in their international relations. It requires all states to settle their international disputes by peaceful means. The principles of the Charter are broad and comprehensive. It is the task of international statesmanship to develop means of international co-operation to make these principles effective. It is difficult for me to believe that a better charter could, in fact, have been agreed upon at San Francisco had the participants had all the

[1] See Address of Secretary of State John Foster Dulles before American Bar Association, August 21, 1953.

4

knowledge of the implications of the nuclear age that we now possess.

The Charter of the United Nations may be far from perfect, but it is the most effective instrument for international co-operation that we have. We should be thankful that President Roosevelt, foreseeing that differences among the Allies would inevitably arise when their enemies were vanquished, wisely insisted that the Charter should be agreed upon before hostilities ceased. And in this instance he had at the time the bipartisan support of Governor Dewey and Mr. Dulles. Had the Charter not been practically completed before the hostilities ceased, it is doubtful whether there would have been a charter. The charter adopted in San Francisco is undoubtedly a better and more workable charter than could have been agreed upon at any time since, notwithstanding the advent of the atomic and hydrogen bombs.

One may say of the Charter, as Chief Justice Marshall said of the Constitution of the United States, that "it was intended to endure for ages to come and to be adapted to the various crises of human affairs"; that it did not "attempt to provide, by immutable rules, for exigencies which, if foreseen at all, must have been seen dimly, and which can best be provided as they occur."[2] Like our Constitution, the Charter was made flexible enough to be adapted to exigencies, which, in the words of Justice Holmes, "could not have been

[2] *McCulloch v. Maryland*, 4 Wheaton 316, 414.

5

completely foreseen by the most gifted of its begetters. It was enough for them to realize or hope that they had created an organism."[3] The Charter laid, and was intended to lay, the broad foundations of an institution capable of life and growth.

The Charter, like our Constitution, sets forth a few basic principles and leaves to those who will live under it the responsibility of finding suitable means of carrying out those principles. Some means are specified in the Charter but these are not necessarily exclusive. The Charter is not a code of legal procedure to be strictly construed. I know no better canon of construction to be used in determining charter power than that laid down by Chief Justice Marshall in *McCulloch v. Maryland*[4] for determining constitutional power: "Let the end be legitimate, let it be within the scope of the Constitution, and all means which are appropriate, which are plainly adapted to that end, which are not prohibited, but consist with the letter and spirit of the Constitution, are constitutional." Member States have the right and responsibility to find means which are appropriate, which are not prohibited but consist with the letter and spirit of the Charter, to carry out the purposes of the Charter.

There is a natural but unfortunate tendency at times to confuse the question of the existence of charter power or competence with the question of the wis-

[3] *Missouri v. Holland*, 252 United States 416, 433.
[4] 4 Wheaton 316, 421.

dom of its exercise. As Justice Holmes has observed: "We fear to grant power and are unwilling to recognize it when it exists."[5] There is scarcely any power that cannot be unwisely exercised. If power or competence is denied for fear of abuse, power to act wisely and prudently may also be lacking. Judgment and statesmanship cannot be secured by restrictive rules, and anarchy is not an adequate substitute for human judgment. The absence of power may save fools from their folly, but its absence may also deny to statesmen the necessary means to make the Charter serve its essential purposes when international peace and security are at stake.

There has been much controversy and debate as to the competence and power of various organs of the United Nations. There have been few Member States which have not altered and shifted their views to conform with their interests, real or imagined, in particular cases. But, generally speaking, charter interpretations that would seriously retard the organic growth and development of the Charter have not prevailed.

* * *

It is interesting to recall that one of the first questions of power arose under the Charter in connection with the power of the Security Council to act when one of its permanent members abstained from voting. Article 27, paragraph 3, of the Charter provides that deci-

[5] *Tyson & Bro. v. Banton,* 273 United States 415, 445 (1927).

sions of the Security Council on matters other than procedure shall be made on the affirmative vote of seven members, including the concurring votes of the permanent members. Many of the early commentators uncritically accepted the view expressed by some of the American Delegation at San Francisco that the abstention of a permanent member should be considered as equivalent to a negative vote or veto. This view was based, as I understand it, on the hope and belief that the Security Council would function most effectively if the permanent members affirmatively supported and accepted responsibility for the Council's acts.

This is a good illustration of Justice Holmes's dictum that even the most gifted begetters of a constitution cannot completely foresee the exigencies which may arise under it. It was one thing to envisage how the Charter might operate if the Great Powers worked harmoniously together. It was quite another thing to limit constitutional power to a preferred procedure that would not work in the absence of such an ideal harmony. Even as a literal interpretation of the Charter, this restrictive view was highly questionable. For the same paragraph of the Charter that provides that decisions of the Council other than procedural shall be made by the affirmative vote of seven members, including the concurring votes of the permanent members, contains a proviso that a party to a dispute under Chapter VII shall abstain from voting. It is certainly self-evident that an abstention required by the Charter was not intended to operate as a veto. Neither the language of the Charter, considering the paragraph in question as a whole, nor logic, nor common sense, was or could be adduced for giving an effect to a voluntary abstention different from the effect given to a compulsory abstention. A state, like an individual, may ordinarily waive its legal rights. Obviously the reasons for allowing a permanent member to waive its right to vote overwhelmingly outweighs any arguments to the contrary. Adequate protection against a rump vote is provided by the Charter requirement of an affirmative vote of seven members.

In the very early days of the Security Council, it became apparent that a permanent member might, for political reasons, be unwilling to vote in favor of a resolution, yet might have no desire to exercise its right of veto, and the competence of the Security Council to act without the concurring vote of an abstaining permanent member was recognized. So salutary is the rule now regarded that the General Assembly has urged the permanent members not to exercise their veto but to accept the decision of a majority of seven on certain agreed categories of nonprocedural questions, such as, for example, the admission of new members.[6] It is such developments as these that should warn us against making snap or abstract judgments on matters of charter power based on a superficial reading

[6] General Assembly Resolution 267 (III), April 14, 1949.

9

of an isolated paragraph or sentence of the Charter or on fragmentary quotations from the Dumbarton Oaks and San Francisco reports.

The rule that voluntary abstention from voting on the part of a permanent member does not prevent the Security Council from taking action has been extended to give the same effect to failure to vote due to voluntary absence. The rule was so extended and applied first when the Soviet Union withdrew from the Council during the discussion of the Iranian case in March 1946. Its most significant application occurred when the Council, in the absence of the Soviet Union, called for collective action to repel the invasion of South Korea in June 1950. A contrary interpretation of the Charter would enable any one of the permanent members to prevent the Security Council from functioning continuously as contemplated by Article 28, paragraph 1, of the Charter. Indeed, it would enable any one of the permanent members to render the Security Council impotent to act in any substantive way at any time by boycotting the proceedings and refusing to participate therein. The naked words of the Charter may be susceptible of various interpretations but to effectuate the Charter's purposes it seems not unreasonable to consider "the concurring votes of the permanent members" as meaning the concurring votes of the permanent members who participate in the voting.[7]

[7] See McDougal and Gardner, "The Veto and the Charter, an Interpretation for Survival," *Yale Law Journal*, 60: 258 (1951); *contra* Leo Gross, "Voting in the Security Council, Abstention for Voting and Absence from Meetings," *Yale Law Journal*, 60: 209 (1951).

The pains of growth are even more evident in the struggle of the Security Council to determine whether a question is a procedural or a nonprocedural question. Article 27 provides that decisions of the Council on *procedural* matters shall be made by an affirmative vote of seven members and that decisions on *all other* matters shall be made by an affirmative vote of seven members, including the concurring votes of the permanent members. There may be reasonable debate as to the proper interpretation and application of the Charter text, but the issue is further complicated by the statement of the Four Sponsoring Powers, China, the Soviet Union, the United Kingdom, and the United States, at the San Francisco Conference in 1945. This statement was not accepted by or voted upon by the San Francisco Conference. At best, it would be binding only on the Four Powers, and even as to them it is questionable how far their ratification of the Charter binds them to a different interpretation from that accepted by other members or how far they can maintain for themselves an interpretation of the text different from that of other members. Be that as it may, the Four Power Statement put a very restrictive gloss on what might be embraced within the concept of procedural matters. While averring that "it will be unlikely that there will arise in the future any matter of great importance on which a decision will have to be made as to whether a procedural vote would apply," the statement proceeded to declare that "should, however, such a matter arise, the decision regarding the preliminary question as to whether or not such matter is procedural must be taken by a vote of seven members of the Security Council including the concurring votes of the permanent members."

Indeed it has been argued with considerable dialectic skill that even apart from the Four Power Statement, the preliminary question as to whether a matter is procedural or not is *not* itself a procedural question. This is the question of the so-called double veto.[8] I should have thought, however, that, without the Four Power Statement, the Security Council would have had little difficulty in treating the preliminary question as a question to be determined by the presiding officer, who may make his own ruling subject to being overruled on a point of order or who may submit the question to the Council to be determined by a procedural vote.

To reduce the area of possible disagreement and conflict with the Four Power Statement, the Assembly, in April 1949, urged that thirty-five categories of questions in an annexed list originally prepared by the Interim Committee be deemed procedural and recommended "that members of the Security Council conduct their business accordingly."[9] In September 1950 the Security Council declined to upset its President's ruling, over the objection of a permanent member,

---

[8] See Leo Gross, "The Double Veto and the Four Power Statement in the Security Council," *Harvard Law Review*, 67: 251 (1953), and "The Question of Laos and the Double Veto in the Security Council," *American Journal of International Law*, 54: 118 (1960).
[9] General Assembly Resolution 267 (III).

that an invitation to the Peking government to a hearing on the Formosa case was a procedural question. In September 1959 the Security Council likewise sustained its President's ruling over similar objection that the creation of a subcommittee, considered to be a subsidiary organ, to report on the complaint of Laos was a procedural matter. Both these questions, it was argued, came within the list of questions deemed procedural in the Assembly's resolution of April 1949.

Existing precedents therefore go far to limit any abuse in the exercise of any so-called double veto. While the views of an objecting permanent member are entitled to respect in case of genuine doubt, and while an objecting permanent member should be allowed to reserve its legal rights, neither the words nor spirit of the Charter require that the judgment of one permanent member should make a question of procedure a question of substance when seven of the other members in good faith conclude that it is clearly a question of procedure.[10]

While the authors of the Four Power Statement undoubtedly wanted to encourage Great Power harmony and unanimity, they failed to realize that you do not get harmony and unanimity simply by requiring it as a condition precedent to any action. Indeed it is too often assumed that when unanimity is required under the Charter and you do not get it, a decision has been taken in favor of the minority; in fact, of course, there

[10] Rudzinski, "The So-Called Double Veto," *American Journal of International Law*, 45: 443 (1951).

has been no decision. Whatever may have been the intent of the draftsmen, the Four Power Statement does not state that, in the absence of unanimity among the permanent members, the preliminary question shall be deemed substantive and not procedural. It does not state that the question shall be considered substantive even though all but one permanent member vote otherwise. The Four Power Statement simply leaves us, when there is no unanimity among the permanent members, with no decision, one way or other. The Statement fails to state expressly what happens when the permanent members fail to agree whether the question is substantive or procedural. It is not suprising or regrettable that the Security Council has followed a less negative course than that suggested by the Four Power Statement and one that is better calculated to promote the purposes and principles of the Charter.

* * *

It is true that during the Dumbarton Oaks and San Francisco Conferences, great emphasis—excessive emphasis—was placed on the unity of the five Great Powers as the basis of the new world order to be created by the Charter. Undoubtedly the impression then was current that the United Nations would not be able to function in the absence of Great Power unity. I recall touring the western states with a small group to explain the Dumbarton Oaks draft. Whenever we were asked what would happen if the Great Powers could not agree, one of our group would arise and explain that Great Power unity was essential to the successful functioning of the Charter, and we must strive with determination and confidence to achieve it because there could be no United Nations if the Great Powers did not work together. I would then rise, and, recalling Chief Justice Marshall's great canon of constitutional construction, express a different point of view. I would stress the fact that under the Charter all members—the great, as well as the smaller, states— obligated themselves to act in accordance with the purposes and principles of the Charter. The Charter provided certain means of enforcement but if these failed, due to disagreement among the Great Powers, other means consistent with the purposes and principles of the Charter would have to be, and would and could be, found to uphold the law of the Charter.

Despite the emphasis placed at that time on the importance of Great Power unity, our government took the position during the very first year of the United Nations, as Ambassador Austin stated in a memorable address before the General Assembly on October 30, 1946:

"The unanimity requirement in the Security Council does not relieve the permanent members from any of the responsibilities and obligations they have assumed under the Charter. . . . The permanent members are bound legally and morally in the same degree

15

as all other members of the United Nations to settle their international dispute by peaceful means in such a manner that international peace and security are not endangered: In the same degree as other members, they are bound to 'refrain from the threat or use of force against the territorial integrity or political independence of any state or in any manner inconsistent with the purposes of the United Nations.' These sweeping and binding commitments are not limited by the power of veto in the Security Council. The veto does not legalize any violations of these commitments. They are the law."

Earlier in the same address Ambassador Austin stated:

"The General Assembly wields power primarily as the voice of the conscience of the world. Its recommendations have behind them the intangible force of the world community. The peace-loving states which are members of the United Nations will not lightly disregard or flout recommendations which express the will of an alert and aroused public opinion. . . . Under the broad and flexible construction of the Charter which the United States wishes to develop, we foresee a great and expanding area of operations for the General Assembly."

It is, of course, true that the draftsmen of the Charter gave primary responsibility for the maintenance of security to the Security Council and undoubtedly generally contemplated that threats to the peace would be dealt with by the Security Council with the concurrence of the five Great Powers. Many for that reason mistakenly assumed that nothing could be done and that the Charter would fall apart if the Great Powers could not agree. They ignored the fact that it was primary and not exclusive jurisdiction which was given to the Security Council to deal with threats to the peace, and that the General Assembly had a broad range of competence in this field. Experience has demonstrated that the founding fathers builded better than many had assumed and that the Charter can function and even collective security measures can be instituted by the General Assembly in the absence of agreement among the Great Powers.

The Uniting for Peace Resolution adopted by the General Assembly in 1950 provides the basis for voluntary co-operation of member states to carry out the General Assembly's recommendations for the maintenance of peace and security when the Security Council is unable to act because of the failure or inability of the permanent members to agree. This resolution was adopted by the General Assembly a few months after the Security Council, in the absence of the Soviet Union, had called for collective action to repel the invasion of South Korea. It served to make clear that United Nations intervention in Korea did not depend solely on the fortuitous absence of Soviet Union from the Security Council, but could and would have been authorized by the General Assembly, had the Soviet

Union been present and vetoed action by the Security Council.

The Uniting for Peace Resolution affirms the competence of the General Assembly, when the Security Council is unable to act in any case of a threat to or breach of peace or act of aggression, to make recommendations for collective measures to maintain or restore peace, including in the case of a breach of peace or act of aggression the use of armed force.[11] The Uniting for Peace Resolution is a great constitutional landmark in the development of the Charter comparable to Marshall's decision in *McCulloch v. Maryland.*

The discovery of alternate ways of uniting for peace under the Charter may be likened to the discovery of alternate ways of approving treaties under our own Constitution. Not only can the President make treaties by and with the consent of the Senate, two thirds of the Senators present concurring, but, as we have discovered under the pressure of events, he can in many areas make comparable agreements when they are authorized or approved by simple majorities of both houses of Congress.[12]

The Uniting for Peace Resolution revealed that more could be accomplished within the present framework of the Charter to obviate the difficulties of the veto than could be accomplished by a whole host of amendments that had been proposed for the same purpose.

[11] General Assembly Resolution 377 (V).
[12] Hackworth, *Digest of International Law*, V, (1943), 390.

The fact that the Assembly under the Charter is not competent to command, but can only recommend, measures, does not, in the world as it is, seriously impair the effective authority of the General Assembly. The effectiveness of a request addressed to sovereign states jealous of their power, whether this request be made by the Security Council or the General Assembly, depends not upon whether the request is legally a command or recommendation. It depends not merely on the number of votes recorded in its favor. It depends primarily upon the extent to which the request expresses the reasoned will and elicits the support of an alert and aroused world-wide conscience. In case of disagreement among the Great Powers, Assembly action in some ways is to be preferred to Security Council action which may turn on the votes of nonpermanent members chosen not because they best represent or express world opinion but because, under the practice of geographic distribution and rotation of membership, it happens to be their turn to sit on the Council.

* * *

Of all controversies concerning charter interpretation the most persistent has been that revolving about the effect of paragraph 7 of Article 2 of the Charter on the competence of United Nations organs. That paragraph provides:

"Nothing contained in this present Charter shall authorize the United Nations to intervene in matters which are essentially within the domestic juris-

19

diction of any State or shall require the Members to submit such matters to settlement under the Charter, but this principle shall not prejudice the application of enforcement measures under Chapter VII."

Some have attempted to construe this provision as imposing substantial limitations on what would otherwise be the competence and power of United Nations organs to consider matters that are in fact of international concern and affect vitally the friendly relations of states. Others have taken the view that the provision is in aid, and not in derogation, of the essential purposes and principles of the Charter. They regard the provision merely as an injunction against prying into the domestic affairs of states when they have no significant bearing on matters of international concern. They do not believe the provision was intended to curtail the authority of United Nations organs to deal with matters of genuine international concern simply because they may have originally arisen out of matters within the domestic jurisdiction of a state. There are probably significant differences within these two schools of thought, which not only represent different legal interpretations of the words of the Charter provision, but reflect varying attitudes and opinions as to what matters are of genuine international concern. The adherents of both schools of thought seek support in the statements made in the course of debate at San Francisco. But the San Francisco debates are ambiguous and equivocal because of the ambivalent intent of the participants who did not want to deprive the United Nations of the necessary power and authority to inquire into all matters importantly affecting international peace but, at the same time, desired to say something to allay fears that the United Nations would pry into matters which states would like to think were their exclusive concern.[13]

I share generally the point of view of the school that believes that the Charter should be construed as a whole. I would not ascribe a meaning to paragraph 7 of Articles 2 that would substantially derogate from the authority of the United Nations to carry out the essential purposes and principles of the Charter, and would in practice render largely nugatory and illusory many other provisions of the Charter such as those on human rights and fundamental freedoms. It is my view that paragraph 7 of Article 2 was not intended to take away powers granted to the United Nations by the Charter, but to provide a guide for their construction. The provision has much the same character and effect as the Tenth Amendment of our own Constitution which declares that powers not delegated to the United States are reserved to the States and to the people. Like the Tenth Amendment, Article 2, paragraph 7, of the Charter in effect affirms that the authority of the United Nations does not extend, and should not be

13 See Francis O. Wilcox and Carl M. Marcy, *Proposals for Changes in the United States* (Washington, D. C.: The Brookings Institution, 1955), p. 263.

construed to extend, beyond the powers enumerated in the Charter, but it does not cut down or abridge those powers.

While there has been some inconsistency in the application of Article 2, paragraph 7, by the various organs of the United Nations and by the same organ on different occasions, and considerable inconsistency in the position taken by the Member States on different occasions, the practice has been against giving any unduly restrictive effect or meaning to the Article. There has been some complaint that greater use has not been made of the International Court of Justice in the application of Article 2, paragraph 7. But at San Francisco the right of each organ to interpret its functions and powers was recognized.[14] The question of what is or is not essentially within the domestic jurisdiction of a state cannot be determined by an abstract legal formula. It depends upon an appraisal of the factual situation from which a political judgment cannot be wholly excluded. Experienced statesmen may be better able than learned jurists to gauge the international ramifications and repercussions which stem from situations originating within the domestic jurisdiction of a state, to determine whether such situations have become matters of genuine international concern. As the late Judge Lauterpacht has stated:

"The expression 'essentially, within the domestic

[14] See Leland M. Goodrich, *The United Nations* (New York, 1959), pp. 70 and 76.

jurisdiction of any state' is one capable of divergent interpretations. It seems that expression was deliberately substituted for that used in Article 15(8) of the Covenant which referred to matters which, *according to international law,* are exclusively within the domestic jurisdiction of the State. The change was apparently due to the belief that the body of International Law on the subject is 'indefinite and inadequate' and that to the extent that the matter is dealt with by international practice and by text writers, the conceptions are inadequate and not of a character which ought to be frozen into the new Organization."[15]

Moreover, the question that arises, when Article 2, paragraph 7, is invoked is not simply whether the matter is one of essentially domestic jurisdiction but whether the action proposed constitutes "intervention." Even though the matter be essentially domestic in character, as, for example, a matter concerning labor standards, the Charter does not forbid action with respect to it so long as the action does not constitute intervention.

To quote further from Lauterpacht:

"The exclusion of the right of 'intervention' on the part of the United Nations must be interpreted by reference to the accepted technical meaning of that term. It excludes intervention conceived as dictatorial, mandatory, interference intended to exercise direct

15 *Oppenheim's International Law,* 8th ed. H. Lauterpacht, ed., 2 vols. (Longman's Green, New York, 1955), pp. 414–415.

23

pressure upon the State concerned. It does not rule out action by way of discussion, study, enquiry and recommendation falling short of intervention. . . .

"In so far as a 'recommendation,' although not implying a legal obligation to accept it, is calculated to exercise direct pressure, likely to be followed by measures of enforcement, upon a State in a matter which is essentially within its domestic jurisdiction, it is probable that it would come within the terms of Article 2(7). Other recommendations, even if addressed to individual States, are not excluded by the terms of that provision. The same applies to recommendations which are general in character."[16]

It is not clear just what sort of recommendations Judge Lauterpacht would consider "calculated to exercise direct pressure, likely to be followed by measures of enforcement, upon a State in a matter which is essentially within its domestic jurisdiction." Any recommendation addressed to an individual state is a kind of pressure, but is it "intervention"? If Judge Lauterpacht meant to exclude recommendations that call for sanctions against a particular state or states by other states, I would agree. But other writers have suggested that recommendations may constitute intervention under Article 2, paragraph 7, if the recommendations are addressed not to all members but to particular offending states and call upon them to take specific remedial action or seek to allocate blame to them for

[16] *Ibid.*, pp. 415–416.

failing to do so.[17] Although one form of recommendation may be less wise or less expedient than another in a particular situation, I do not see the basis in Article 2, paragraph 7, for excluding recommendations as constituting intervention unless they call for sanctions.

While divergent interpretations of Article 2, paragraph 7, may be possible, it would seem unfortunate if that paragraph were to be construed to debar states from doing in and through the United Nations what they are not debarred by international law or the Charter from doing separately or collectively outside of the United Nations.

Take the troublesome Algerian question. Of course if it became a threat to, or caused a breach of, international peace within the meaning of Article 39 of Chapter VII, the Security Council could take cognizance of it. But should Article 2, paragraph 7, be construed to deny the Security Council the power to consider it at an earlier stage if the Council finds in the language of Article 34 of Chapter VI that "the continuance of the dispute or situation is likely to endanger the maintenance of international peace or security"? Or should the General Assembly, if the Security Council is not dealing with the situation, be denied the power to consider the situation if in the language of Article 15 of Chapter IV the situation is one which the Assembly "deems likely to impair the general welfare or friendly relations among nations"?

[17] Goodrich, *The United Nations*, p. 79.

To be sure, it may be wise for the Council or the Assembly to defer, as the Assembly has on occasions, discussions of the situation in the hope that deferment will facilitate peaceful settlement. But that is quite different from maintaining that unless and until the Algerian situation has become an imminent threat to international peace under Chapter VII, it must be considered an internal French problem not appropriate for discussion, mediation, or recommendation by the United Nations.

I do not think it will make for peace and a lessening of tensions in the world if a question like the Algerian question is regarded as appropriate for discussion by the American Ambassador in Paris or by a NATO conference in Europe or by a Bandung conference in Asia, but not as appropriate for discussion in the United Nations. Nor do I believe that our government helped France or world peace when it failed to bring —and discouraged others from bringing—to the attention of the United Nations the war in Indo-China. Discussion, formal and informal, at the United Nations, while at times unpleasant, tedious, and trying, may throw more light on the international ramifications and repercussions of supposedly localized events than discussion in any other forum.

In the not distant future, it is possible that it will appear paradoxical that states with colonial interests should have tried to narrow the competence of United Nations organs by an expansive interpretation of the reservations contained in Article 2(7). The colonial powers now fear that dependent people are demanding independence before they have acquired a political maturity which would enable them to cope with the perplexities of modern government. The colonial powers have reason to be concerned that there should prevail in countries emerging from colonial rule a decent respect for human rights and fundamental freedoms, including the rights of minorities to be secure in their person and enjoy the equal protection of law in respect to their person and property. For good or ill, colonialism is passing, and it is not in the interest of international peace and good will for the states which have the most at stake to whittle down the authority of the United Nations to examine the observance of the pledge of all its members to promote respect for and observance of human rights and fundamental freedoms for all without distinction as to race, sex, language, or religion.[18]

* * *

In considering the potentialities of growth under the Charter, it is important to bear in mind that the competence and powers of United Nations organs may derive not only from the Charter but from treaties and *ad hoc* agreements. The Italian Peace Treaty, for ex-

[18] See Abi-Saab, "The Newly Independent States and the Scope of Domestic Jurisdiction," *Proceedings of American Society for International Law* (1960), pp. 84–90.

ample, provided that if the principal Allied Powers did not agree upon the disposition of the Italian colonies within a year, their future status should be determined by the recommendations of the General Assembly, and the Powers concerned agreed to accept and put into effect such recommendations. The same treaty also gave the Security Council protective powers over the Free Territory of Trieste, although the failure of the permanent members to agree upon a governor for the Free Territory led to delays and disputes which were finally resolved by a division of the territory between Italy and Yugoslavia. But the precedents clearly establish the legitimacy and the propriety of enlarging the competence and powers of organs of the United Nations by treaties and agreements that fit into the general framework of the Charter and are not inconsistent with specific provisions of the Charter or its purposes and principles. It is significant to recall that in 1950 the United States tentatively suggested that the Japanese Peace Treaty might provide that if the principal Allied Powers could not agree within one year on the disposition of the territories surrendered, their future status should be determined by the General Assembly. It may possibly be regretted that our government felt compelled by the Korean War not to persist in this suggestion, but instead took upon itself unilaterally the responsibility for the maintenance of peace in the Formosan area.

Some of the gaps which some have believed existed

in the Charter can perhaps more appropriately and satisfactorily be filled out by specific treaties and agreements than by formal charter amendments or by a general revision of the Charter. It may, for example, be desirable that the United Nations should have greater power and authority in the field of disarmament. It seems highly doubtful, however, whether that power and authority could be incorporated in any succinct general amendment which would be workable and effective and at the same time elicit the necessary agreement. But if the states having substantial armaments could agree on carefully safeguarded disarmament agreements, there is no reason why such agreements cannot and should not give to organs of the United Nations, either to those now in being or to others to be created, powers of supervision and enforcement. Such agreements, to which all states would be invited and encouraged to adhere, could commit the parties thereto to respect the recommendations and findings made by the designated United Nations organs in accordance with agreed voting procedures, which could dispense with any veto to the extent provided by the agreements. True, it may be difficult to induce the Great Powers to waive the veto in such agreements, but the chances of inducing them to do so in situations clearly defined in the agreements would probably be far better than the chances of inducing them to waive the veto generally, or even in the broad field of arms control, by general charter amendment.

29

It is not the Charter which impedes the expansion of United Nations activities in disarmament and arms control, or in other areas affecting international peace and security, but a lack of a working consensus among the Member States. The Charter has created an organism capable of life and growth, but that life and growth depends not only on the words of the Charter but on the way Member States meet their responsibilities and exercise their rights and privileges under the Charter. We will consider in the next chapter some of the responsibilities of Member States under the Charter and how in significant situations those responsibilities have been met.

Chapter 2

Responsibilities
of Member States
Under the Charter

IN MY FIRST chapter I reviewed successive precedents which have gone far to establish the broad competence of organs of the United Nations to deal with situations and disputes which may seriously affect international peace and security. But competence or power to act does not ensure a requisite consensus or wise action. Agreement on what action is wise is all the more difficult when competence to act is not competence to command action or to compel compliance but only to recommend action or compliance by Member States. The United Nations is not a supra-national organization, but an organization or instrumentality through which sovereign states can voluntarily cooperate with a view to their common interests in international peace, security, and law.

The Charter makes possible the life and growth of the United Nations, but how the United Nations develops and grows depends not so much on the words of the Charter as on the way Member States exercise their rights and privileges and meet their responsibilities under the Charter.

If the United Nations is to live and grow, Member States must not only observe their obligations under the Charter, but exercise their rights under the Charter wisely and prudently. The future of the United Nations may be compromised by the non-use or the unwise use by Member States of their charter powers.

It does not follow from the fact that the United Nations has competence or power to consider a situation that the United Nations ought invariably to discuss it at length or pass a resolution concerning it. The existence of jurisdiction does not make mandatory its exercise. It is a task of statesmanship—often a very difficult one—to determine whether the exercise of power will relieve or aggravate a situation. The right of a Member State to bring a situation to the attention of the General Assembly or Security Council should not oblige either organ to open up the question for full-dress debate or even necessarily to put it formally on the Agenda, if on preliminary consideration such action is deemed unwise at the time. For example, it would not have been desirable to open up the Algerian question to full-dress debate on the eve of a meeting between DeGaulle and Ferhat Abbas. Flexible and varied procedures and practices are required for dealing with the many and diverse situations which may come within the competence of the United Nations. The question of jurisdictional power should not be confused with the wisdom of exercising or refraining from exercising that power or with the question of the wisdom of exercising that power in a particular way. Rules of competence and constitutional power can afford no substitute for statesmanship on the part of Member States.

Of course, when the United Nations has competence in a delicate situation in which it has no power to compel corrective action, Member States should proceed cautiously so as to encourage a favorable response to, and not a strong reaction against, United Nations efforts. Serious responsibility rests upon Member States to avoid couching their proposed recommendations in a form which may not only result in their being ignored but may, in fact, in certain situations, create greater intransigeance on the part of those criticized and worsen the situation of those most deserving of sympathy and support. But an appreciation of practical difficulties should not be exploited as an easy escape from the responsibilities of statesmanship which must be exercised by Member States.

Indeed, discretion is not always the better part of valor. In critical situations involving great national and international tensions, there is bound to be resentment and protest not only if the Member States vote to consider and debate the issues but if they sidetrack dis-

33

cussion and debate of the issues. Resentment and protest do not necessarily mean that United Nations deliberations and recommendations are futile. On the contrary resentment and protest may reflect the political impact of the United Nations deliberations. In retrospect the United Nations deliberations on the Cyprus question appeared to have helped clarify the issues and to have facilitated the ultimate settlement, although many doubted the constructive value of the activities of the United Nations until the settlement was actually achieved.

There has sometimes been objection to United Nations consideration of the problem of race relations in South Africa on the ground that United Nations debate and resolutions only arouse resentment on the part of the government and the electorate in South Africa. But it should be recognized that the United Nations actions give encouragement and help to those elements in South Africa desiring to bring about change by lawful means and may not be without impact on the government and those who support the policies of apartheid. It ought not to be forgotten that the elimination of moderate political opposition leads almost inexorably to revolution by extremists. If the United Nations by its deliberations in the General Assembly and Security Council can foster and promote evolutionary change in South Africa before it is too late for anything but violent revolution, a great good will have been accomplished.

Unfortunately in recent years there has been a perceptible decline in the use of the organs of the United Nations for peaceful settlement of disputes. This cannot be ascribed to the Charter but to a changed attitude on the part of important Member States. Contrast the vigor with which the question of Indonesian independence was handled in the early days of the United Nations with the failure of the United Nations a few years later even to attempt to deal with the problem of Indo-China. Our government has evinced little or no interest in exploring the Soviet suggestion of introducing a United Nations presence in Berlin. It may have been only a ruse on the part of the Soviet Union to get Allied troops out of Berlin. Be that as it may, no counter-suggestion for the utilization of a United Nations presence to strengthen the freedom and independence of Berlin has been made. It is extraordinary that there is no recognition of the United Nations interest and concern in the threats to international peace in Laos.

The sidetracking and soft-pedalling of the pacific settlement functions of the United Nations may be ascribed in large part to the Cold War. Issues formally brought to the United Nations for peaceful settlement have been exploited for propaganda purposes and serious efforts to harmonize differences have been noticeable by their absence. The mediation and conciliation functions of the United Nations have been neglected and allowed to atrophy.

Dogmatic judgments about by-passing the United Nations should not be made. But it is clear that the United Nations cannot be an effective instrument in the maintenance of peace and security if the Great Powers keep vital issues which threaten the peace away from the United Nations until they actually erupt into war.

The United Nations is not a totalitarian institution. The Charter does not require all international action to be done in or through the United Nations. The Charter (Article 33) expressly urges parties to disputes to seek their solution by peaceful means of their own choice. But the Charter provides no excuse for Member States' keeping their disputes from the United Nations after they have failed to settle them outside the United Nations when the disputes are of a character to threaten the maintenance of peace.

* * *

The by-passing of the pacific settlement functions of the United Nations cannot be excused because of the inability of the Great Powers to agree upon the implementation of Article 43, which was intended to make available to the Security Council armed forces of Member States. The lack of agreement among the Great Powers which had rendered Article 43 inoperative may necessitate and justify collective defense arrangements like NATO, but such arrangements cannot supplant the peaceful settlement functions of the United Nations.

Regional and collective defense arrangements are lawful under Article 51 and 52 of the Charter. Such arrangements properly conceived and carried out need not undermine, but can reinforce and support, the Charter. On the whole NATO has helped, not hindered, its members in meeting their responsibilities to the United Nations.

But it is not the form of military arrangements as much as the way they are administered that determines whether in fact they support or weaken the Charter. The military officers who administer some of these arrangements, however, too frequently in their public statements speak as if they were unmindful of any obligations toward the United Nations. They seem to accept the point of view expressed by the late Senator Robert A. Taft that collective security under the United Nations is an unworkable principle and that we have "no choice except to disregard the United Nations and to develop our own military policy and our own policy of alliances without regard to the nonexistent power of the United Nations to prevent aggression"; that we should use the United Nations only as a "diplomatic weapon," and that "we have to engage in our own wars when we think we should engage in them and not at other times."[1] Such thinking ignores our obligations under the Charter, as well as the embarrassments and dangers which confront us if we

---

[1] See speech by Senator Robert A. Taft in the United States Senate, January 5, 1951, *Congressional Record*, Eighty-second Congress, second session, pp. 57, 64.

37

think we can use the United Nations only when it suits our convenience. So long as states adhere to the Charter, they are not free to use the United Nations as a mere diplomatic weapon in the Cold War and to disregard their obligations to refrain from the use of force contrary to the purposes and principles of the Charter.

* * *

This brings us to the question: Just what is the scope and effect of the obligations which paragraphs 3 and 4 of Article 2 of the Charter impose on Member States? These provisions require Member States to settle their disputes by peaceful means in such a manner that international peace and security and justice are not endangered and to refrain from the threat or use of force in any manner inconsistent with the purposes of the Charter. What do these provisions, which are the very heart of the Charter, mean?

It is generally stated that these Charter provisions forbid all resort to armed force with two exceptions: the one being for collective or individual self-defense against armed attack on a Member State within Article 51; and the other for collective action pursuant to competent decisions of United Nations organs. Professor Julius Stone, in his book *Aggression and World Order*,[2] has challenged this generally accepted interpretation. He contends that Article 2, paragraph 4,

[2] *Aggression and World Order: Critique of United Nations Theories of Aggression* (University of California, 1958), pp. 93–103.

38

does not unqualifiedly forbid the use of force but only the use of force in a manner inconsistent with the purposes of the United Nations which envisage effective collective measures to bring about adjustment or settlement of grievances "in conformity with principles of justice and international law." He argues that it would be a strange application of charter principles to require law-abiding members of the Organization to submit indefinitely to admitted and persistent violations of right, particularly when no collective measures are available for the remedy of just grievances.

Professor Milton Katz, in his address before the American Society of International Law at its Fifty-fourth Annual Meeting in April, 1960,[3] sharply differs with Professor Stone. He states that Article 2, paragraphs 3 and 4, constitute an undertaking to refrain from the use of force, and Article 51 provides the sole exception, reserving to members the right to use armed force in self-defense against armed attack by another state. He concedes that in a limited number of cases a member forbidden to resort to self-help may obtain redress from the Security Council or General Assembly by establishing that the conduct of the offending state creates a threat to the peace within the meaning of Article 39 or a situation likely to endanger international peace and security within the meaning of Article 11. But then he proceeds to state that except within

[3] See *Proceedings of American Society of International Law* (1960), pp. 254–256.

39

these narrow limits neither the Charter as presently construed and applied, nor any other aspect of contemporary international law, provides means of redress. He concedes that this is unjust and impracticable, and in the long run cannot endure, and asserts that if the prohibitions against the use of armed force are to be maintained, as they must, the area vacated by force must be filled by law.

I agree with Professor Katz that the Charter forbids the use of force except for individual or collective self-defense against armed attack under Article 51 or for collective measures authorized by competent organs of the United Nations. Professor Stone's interpretation of the Charter would come near making the Charter prohibition of the use of force illusory and meaningless in practice. But I cannot agree with Professor Katz that except in a very limited number of cases a member deprived by the Charter of the right of self-help is denied all other means of redress for its injuries and grievances.

The Charter not only requires members to refrain from the use of force in their international relations [Article 2 (4)]. It also requires them to settle their disputes by peaceful means in such manner that international peace and security and justice are not endangered [Article 2 (3)]. A state which resorts to force to redress its grievances violates the law of the Charter. But a state which refuses to consider the serious grievances of a sister state and refuses to agree to any procedure for their peaceful settlement also violates the law of the Charter. The provisions of the Charter are interrelated and interdependent. Force is proscribed as a means of settlement, but members must be willing to submit their disputes for settlement under some reasonable procedure. I believe that the United Nations, when it intervenes, as it should intervene to preserve the peace, should call upon all parties concerned to fulfill their obligations under the Charter and should frame its recommendations not only to stop the fighting but to provide that minimal relief of grievances which may be necessary or appropriate to prevent the renewal of the strife. While the primary purpose of the United Nations must be to maintain peace, peace cannot be maintained solely by forbidding the use of force without some minimal redress of genuine grievances. While I am most sympathetic with Professor Katz's plea for intensified efforts toward the progressive development of international law, I do not think that the Charter leaves us with as complete a vacuum in the meanwhile as he apparently believes.

It seems to me that it is much more important to recognize the constitutional responsibility of the United Nations organs to prescribe a minimal redress of grievances when they intervene to preserve the peace than to engage in a dialectic debate as to the limits of the right of self-redress. The important point is that the United Nations has authority to restore and maintain peace. The United Nations has authority to restore peace when force is used in self-defense under Article 51. It has authority to intervene even in a civil war or

41

in the case of alleged indirect aggression in situations like Laos, Lebanon, and Guatemala, if the conflict constitutes a threat to international peace.

The primary task of the United Nations is to maintain and restore peace on a tolerable and endurable basis and not to assess blame or comparative fault. Whether the resort to force by one state against another is lawful or unlawful, no state against which force is applied should be relieved for that reason of its obligations to settle its disputes by peaceful means in such a manner that international peace and security, and justice, are not endangered. On the other hand, the failure of one Member State to agree to settle its disputes with another Member State by peaceful means should not relieve the latter state of its obligation to refrain from the use of force, but should enable that state to obtain such redress as can be given by the Security Council or General Assembly in situations involving a threat to the peace. When a state refuses to consider any procedure for the settlement of a dispute which another state contends seriously affects its vital interests, the organs of the United Nations should not hesitate to regard such a situation as a threat to the peace without requiring the state aggrieved to resort to an unlawful show of force. Even the English common law was flexible enough to dispense with proof of force and arms in case of direct trespass. It certainly would not make sense for the United Nations to deny relief to an aggrieved state on the ground that there was no threat to the peace; and then if the aggrieved state threatened the peace to obtain relief, for the United Nations to deny relief because the show of force was forbidden by the Charter. There should be no vacuum unless the United Nations fails to provide relief.

Except, therefore, in the clearest case of self-defense against armed attack, Member States have, and should have, no right to resort to force without invoking the assistance of the United Nations to secure a redress of their grievances.

* * *

The Suez affair, culminating in the Anglo-French-Israeli action against Egypt in the fall of 1956, should serve as a warning of the danger of thinking that security measures involving the use of armed forces except in the clearest cases of self-defense can safely be carried out without reference to the United Nations and the obligations of member states under the Charter. The British and French made the same error that Senator Taft made. They assumed that because security preparations outside of the United Nations were necessary, security operations involving the use of armed force could also be conducted outside of and without regard to the United Nations.

The British and French governments announced in advance an airborne invasion of the Suez Canal zone with the professed object of separating the Israeli and Egyptian forces and protecting the Canal from the hostilities. While neither France nor Britain attempted to conceal its vital interest in the Canal, it was obvious that they were attempting to assume international policing or collective security functions without consultation with the United Nations. The United States not being directly involved and apparently not being consulted, regarded the action as extremely ill advised apart from the merits of the controversy.

The tactical blunders, diplomatic and military, of the British and French gravely prejudiced their case in the United Nations. The suddenness with which the issue of a breach of the peace, isolated from its causes, was brought to the United Nations, led to a one-sided consideration of the case. The British and French had their grievances against Egypt arising out of the seizure of the Suez Canal in retaliation against the United States's sudden withdrawal of its support from the Aswan Dam project. They did fear grave injury to their vital interest in uninterrupted access to Middle Eastern oil through accustomed transportation routes. Israel had taken up arms with the avowed object of defending herself against fedayeen raids conducted against Israel from bases within the Gaza strip and the Sinai peninsula, resulting in the loss of Israeli lives and properties. Had the United Nations, in response to Israel's complaint, dispatched United Nations guards to patrol the border, as Mr. Adlai Stevenson had suggested in November 1955, there would have been no occasion for Israel to take up arms in self-defense. In any event, it was not necessary for the United Nations to prejudge the merits of the controversy. The United Nations has authority to deal with a threat or breach of peace without regard to which party or parties, or whether any party, is guilty of aggression or a breach of peace.[4] In fact the resolutions of the General Assembly in late 1956 made no finding of aggression or breach of the Charter. But the resolutions did seek not merely to stop the fighting, but to restore the *status quo ante* without making any provision for inquiring into the merits of the controversy. And this did involve, at least by implication, a prejudgment of the case against Britain, France, and Israel. Many of the delegates, particularly members of the Afro-Asian bloc, argued that the United Nations should not even hear or consider the grievances of Britain, France, and Israel until they had purged themselves of their aggression.

Although the resolutions called for the restoration of the *status quo ante*, in fact Israel did not withdraw within the armistice lines until given assurances that the United Nations Emergency Forces would remain in the Gaza strip to guard the border, and would remain at Sharm el Sheikh to prevent the blockade of the Israeli port of Elath on the Gulf of Agaba. Moreover, before withdrawing, Israel sought and obtained assurances from President Eisenhower of American support of the Israel's right of passage through the Suez Canal. Indeed, in the absence of countervailing

[4] See Julius Stone, *Aggression and World Order*, p. 159.

45

force it is not likely that states will obey a cease-fire order or recommendation unless assured of some minimal redress of their grievances. Over the long run the Charter is unlikely to be effective in preventing states feeling aggrieved in their vital interests from taking the law into their own hands if the United Nations, when it seeks to stop a breach of peace, does not bestir itself to consider the grievances—real or alleged—that provoked the fighting and the measures necessary to reduce those grievances to tolerable limits.[5]

* * *

In light of the charter difficulties Britain and France encountered in the Suez affair, it would seem advisable for us to consider whether our unilaterally announced policies in regard to the defense of Formosa and the Pescadores may not under certain circumstances involve us in similar difficulties.

This is all the more important since Ambassador Adlai Stevenson in his first press conference as our United Nations Representative, maintaining prior positions of our government, has declared: "Communist China threats to take Taiwan, by force if necessary, are inconsistent with the renunciation of force which is an obligation of all members of the United Nations."[6] If we are going to call on others—even those whose representation in the United Nations we have opposed—to observe the Charter obligations of Member States, we

[5] *Ibid.,* p. 160.
[6] *New York Times,* January 28, 1961.

46

should be clear as to what those obligations under the Charter are.

This requires first of all some examination of the legal status of Formosa (Taiwan) and the Pescadores. Japan had acquired these islands from China by the Treaty of Shimonoseki in 1895 after the Sino-Japanese War. In the Cairo Declaration of 1943, Roosevelt, Churchill, and Chiang Kai-shek proclaimed that it was their purpose that Formosa and the Pescadores should be restored to the Republic of China. Pursuant to direction of General MacArthur, the Supreme Commander for the Allied Powers, Japan at the close of World War II, surrendered Formosa and the Pescadores to Chiang Kai-shek "acting in behalf of the United States, the Republic of China, the United Kingdom and the British Empire and the Union of Soviet Socialist Republics." Administrative control of the islands was then turned over to the Republic of China in September 1945. Before the Peace Treaty with Japan was drafted and signed, the Chinese Communists succeeded in a civil war in driving Chiang Kai-shek from the mainland of China. Formosa became in fact the seat of the National Government of the Republic of China in December 1949.[7]

On June 27, 1950, following the attack on Korea, President Truman ordered the Seventh Fleet to pre-

---

[7] See Mutual Defense Treaty with the Republic of China, United States Senate Report No. 2, February 8, 1955, Eighty-fourth Congress, first session, p. 6.

47

vent any attack on Formosa and any operations from Formosa against the mainland. At the same time he declared that the determination of the future status of Formosa must await the restoration of security in the Pacific, a peace settlement with Japan, or consideration by the United Nations.[8]

In the summer of 1950, Mr. Dulles prepared a seven-point statement of principles which was to form the basis of a proposed peace treaty with Japan. According to this statement, Japan was to be requested to accept the decision of the United Kingdom, the Soviet Union, China, and the United States with reference to the future status of Formosa and the Pescadores and, in the event there was no agreed decision within a year, the United Nations General Assembly would decide.[9] When, however, the Japanese Treaty was finally adopted, it merely provided for the renunciation by Japan of all rights to Formosa and the Pescadores. In explaining the treaty at the San Francisco Peace Conference on September 5, 1951, Mr. Dulles stated: "We had either to give Japan peace on the Potsdam surrender terms or deny peace to Japan while the allies

[8] See Edwin C. Hoyt, "The United States Reaction to the Korean Attack: A Study in the Principles of the United Nations Charter as a Factor in American Policy-Making," 55 *American Journal of International Law* 45 (January 1961), pp. 62–76.

[9] See Japanese Peace Treaty and Other Treaties Relating to Security in the Pacific, United States Senate Executives A, B, C, and D, January 10, 1952, Eighty-second Congress, second session. For report of the Senate Committee on Foreign Relations, see Executive Report No. 2, February 14, 1952, Eighty-second Congress, second session, pp. 21–22.

quarrel about what should be done with what Japan is prepared, and required, to give up. Clearly the wise course was to proceed now, so far as Japan is concerned, leaving the future to resolve doubts by invoking international solvents other than this treaty."[10]

In his State of the Union Message on February 2, 1953, President Eisenhower stated he was issuing instructions that the Seventh Fleet should no longer be employed to shield Communist China from attack. Chiang Kai-shek, with our help and encouragement, greatly strengthened his position on the small offshore islands, Quemoy, Matsu, and the Tachens—islands only a few miles off the mainland—from which he conducted nuisance and intelligence raids on the mainland and occasional forays against Red China shipping in the area. I mention these facts because they are difficult to reconcile with the stand we might have taken: that as the power responsible for the occupation of Formosa we have a responsibility toward the people of Formosa to see that they were not denied the right of self-determination. The assumption on which the Cairo Declaration was based—that the people of Formosa desired to become a part of China—could not be taken for granted after the changed situation created by the civil war on the mainland. But it was obviously difficult to permit Formosa to be used as a base of operation in China's civil war and still isolate Formosa from the civil war.

[10] See Japanese Peace Treaty . . . , Executives A, B, C, and D, p. 8.

When in 1954 the Red Chinese began to launch attacks against the offshore islands, our policy shifted to the defensive. The Chinese Nationalists agreed not to make armed attacks on the mainland without our consent, and Mr. Dulles made clear our consent was not likely to be forthcoming. In December 1954, a Mutual Defense Treaty was negotiated with Chiang's Republic of China which, subject to termination on a year's notice, committed the United States to the defense of Formosa and the Pescadores, described as territories of the Republic of China. In January 1955, while the ratification of the Treaty was still under consideration, the President requested a Congressional resolution authorizing him to use force to defend Formosa and the Pescadores from armed attack, the authority to include the securing and protection of such related positions and territories in that area now in friendly hands as the President judged to be required or appropriate in the defense of Formosa and the Pescadores. This raised the highly controversial question of the defense of the offshore islands, which, unlike Formosa, had always, prior to the civil war, been inseparable in sovereignty from the mainland.

At a press conference on December 1, 1954, Secretary Dulles was asked whether the treaty recognized the claim of the Nationalists, the Republic of China, to sovereignty over the mainland. He replied: "It does not deal specifically with that matter one way or the other." He informed the Senate Foreign Relations

Committee that "the reference in the treaty to 'the territories of either of the parties' was language carefully chosen to avoid denoting anything one way or the other about their sovereignty." The Senate Committee recorded "the understanding of the Senate that nothing in the treaty should be construed as affecting or modifying the legal status or sovereignty of the territories to which it applies." But the Committee did not attempt to define what that status was beyond asserting: "Both by act and implication we have accepted the Nationalist Government as the lawful authority on Formosa."[11] The Committee also recorded the understanding that "military operations by either party from the territories held by the Republic of China shall not be undertaken except by joint agreement."[12]

There can, I believe, be little doubt, however, that the Republic of China considers itself to be the lawful government of China and considers Formosa to be a province of the Republic of China. The Republic of China is the only government of China recognized by the United States, and at present represents China in the various organs of the United Nations.

Now what is the effect of the Charter and its prohibition of the threat or use of force in international rela-

[11] See Mutual Defense Treaty with the Republic of China, Senate Executive Report No. 2, February 8, 1955, Eighty-fourth Congress, first session, p. 6.

[12] Ibid., p. 4. See also memorandum by the author commenting on the proposed treaty, Congressional Record, Eighty-fourth Congress, second session, p. 101.

tions on this confused and muddled situation? Neither the Charter nor international law forbids civil war as such. But the Charter does authorize the United Nations to intervene if civil war constitutes a threat to international peace.[13] While the Formosan question has come before the United Nations on several occasions, there has been no serious effort to reach a peaceful solution through the United Nations.

If Formosa, including the Pescadores, can be considered to be politically independent and separate from the Chinese mainland, there would be nothing in the Charter to deter us from participating in the collective self-defense of these islands in event of armed attack from the Chinese mainland, unless the armed attack was provoked by an armed attack on the mainland from Formosa. Indeed, having freed Formosa from Japanese rule, we may be said to have a special responsibility to protect the right of the Formosans to a government of their own choice. Moreover, if Formosa is an independent political entity, an armed attack against Formosa by the Peoples' Republic of China would be inconsistent with the obligations of Member States under Article 2, paragraph 4, of the Charter.

On the other hand, if Formosa, including the Pescadores, has become part of China and has passed under the control of a government of China that claims jurisdiction over the mainland, then a war between two rival governments over the possession of Formosa

[13] Hans Kelsen, *The Law of the United Nations* (New York, 1950), p. 19.

would be a civil war. Neither of the rival Chinese governments would in that event be acting contrary to the Charter unless and until the United Nations intervened to stop the fighting on the ground that it constituted a threat to international peace.

But do we have the same liberty under the Charter when our military role involves us in a conflict that has progressed far beyond armed insurrection to a civil war in which the insurgents have extended control over vast territories and have organized that control under a regular government which has achieved a substantial measure of international recognition? It seems doubtful that Article 51 of the Charter recognizes such a right. Although the armed forces of one state may be stationed in the territory of another state on the latter's invitation to assist in the maintenance of order, it is by no means clear that the armed forces of one state may participate in the fighting in another state's civil war on one side or the other without running afoul of Article 2, paragraph 4, of the Charter, forbidding the use of force in international relations in any manner inconsistent with the purposes of the Charter. Professor Quincy Wright, for example, contends:

"International law does not permit the use of force in the territory of another state on invitation either of the recognized or the insurgent government in times of rebellion, insurrection or civil war. Since international law recognizes the right of revolution, it cannot permit the other state to intervene to prevent it. The United Nations itself cannot intervene to stop civil

53

strife unless it concludes that such strife threatens international peace and security or violates an internationally recognized cease-fire line."[14]

If different states recognize and come to the support of different factions in a civil war, the threat to world peace is obvious. Events in Europe in connection with the Spanish Civil War made this obvious. Such are the very dangers which loom ahead in the Congo. We should be slow to commit ourselves to charter interpretations that would gravely weaken the restraints which the Charter imposes on the use of force in international relations. If we believe that organized civil armed conflict affects international peace and security, we may ask the United Nations to intervene. Indeed, we have a duty to do so. But our right on our own responsibility to intervene with force is an entirely different matter.

Now obviously the charter difficulties arise from the uncertain status of Formosa and the Pescadores, and their status is uncertain because the position taken by the government of the United States and by Chiang's Republic of China is ambivalent and equivocal. It seems to me that rather than to defend or bolster up an equivocal and doubtful case, and in the process to commit ourselves to a highly questionable interpretation of the Charter, it would be the part of wisdom for Chiang's government and the government of the United States to make their case clear and unequivocal

[14] See Quincy Wright, "Subversive Intervention," *American Journal of International Law*, 54: 529 (1960), and "United States Intervention in the Lebanon," *ibid.*, 53: 112f (1959).

while there is still time. That can be done by taking steps to make clear beyond cavil that Formosa and the Pescadores constitute an independent state and that its government does not claim to be or to represent the government of the Chinese mainland in the United Nations or elsewhere. Such a course would seem to be in the clear interest of the United States and the people of Formosa and the Pescadores, including the Chinese Nationalists who have found a home there and have contributed significantly to its development.

It would seem that the government of Formosa and the Pescadores—call it the Republic of China in Formosa and the Pescadores if you wish—is able to maintain its independence as a matter of fact and of law from the mainland. In fact it has not as yet been subject to serious attack from the mainland and may not be for some time to come. It is much more difficult to maintain in fact or in law the independence from the mainland of the offshore islands which are within artillery-range of the mainland. Tying the offshore islands to Formosa makes it much more difficult to isolate Formosa from the civil war. Quemoy and Matsu would seem no more essential to the defense of Formosa than the Tachens, which were evacuated by the Chinese Nationalists in 1955.

It is a current prediction in informed United Nations circles that the credentials of the delegates of the People's Republic of China will be accepted in the Sixteenth Annual Meeting of the General Assembly in the fall of 1961, and the delegates from Red China will be accepted as the representatives of China. It would seem very important that before this occurs we should do what we can to induce the Nationalist government in Formosa to declare its independence from the mainland and to bring about its separate membership in the United Nations.

This might be accomplished by the General Assembly's recognizing that two new states have succeeded to the original Republic of China. If both Formosa and the Communist mainland are members of the United Nations, then each would be bound under the Charter to respect the territorial integrity and political independence of the other.

An analysis of the Formosan situation reveals that an appeal to the rule of law does not provide an automatic or inevitable answer to a difficult and delicate political situation. But it does show that wise international statesmanship should combine both a knowledge of law and of politics.

Perhaps I should add here that I think there has also been a lack of coordination between law and diplomacy in the handling of the recent Laotian crisis. That the civil conflict in Laos constitutes a threat to international peace I have no doubt. That gives us the right to ask the United Nations to intervene. But unless there has been an armed attack against Laos by some other state, I doubt whether we have the right under Article 51 to intervene or to threaten to intervene with force on our own unilateral responsibility. I fear that we may be establishing a precedent which, if followed, would seriously weaken the obligations of states under Article 2, paragraph 4, to refrain from the threat or use of force except in self-defense as defined in Article 51. I fear the establishment of such a precedent would not be in the long-term interest of the United States or of the United Nations.

I hope that we are successful in our efforts to obtain a cease-fire in Laos through diplomatic negotiations with the Soviet Union. But if these efforts fail, I hope we seek the assistance of the United Nations in obtaining a cease-fire, and in the meantime avoid taking the law into our own hands lest other nations also take the law into their own hands.

It is difficult to observe the law in a world where there is no assurance of the equal observance of law by all. But let us at least be conscious of what we do, of the dilemma we face, and of the risks we incur, whichever way we turn in the struggle for law.[15]

* * *

The Congo situation has raised the question of the role of the Secretary-General and the degree to which

[15] It is not easy to reconcile our part in the abortive invasion of Cuba, which occurred during the week these lectures were delivered, with our obligations to the United Nations and the Organization of American States. Quite apart from our charter and treaty obligations, our position in the Western Hemisphere and in the world would have been greatly strengthened if we had made a forthright appeal to the United Nations before taking the law into our own hands. We could have truthfully averred that international peace was threatened by a dictatorship in Cuba not responsible to the Cuban people. We could have asked that the Cuban people be allowed to determine their own destiny by free elections under the supervision of the Organization of American States.

the integrity of his office rests upon the support of the Member States. Obviously there is no responsibility upon the part of Member States affirmatively to support positions of the Secretary-General with which they honestly disagree, but there is a great difference between honest dissent and deliberate obstruction and sabotage.

If other organs of the United Nations were functioning, there would be less debate about the role of the Secretary-General. We have observed that the General Assembly has assumed a larger and more important role than the founding fathers had contemplated. This was because the failure of the Great Powers to work together had made it impossible for the Security Council to function as the founding fathers had hoped it would. Similarly, the inability of the General Assembly to spell out the answers to many problems which arise from general action authorized by the General Assembly, has magnified the role of the Secretary-General.

In the Suez affair, as in the more recent Congo affair, the organization and management of the United Nations forces and the United Nations presence have rested largely on the Secretary-General. In both instances the resolutions had to be hastily prepared, and the Secretary-General has had to deal with many delicate problems without much guidance or help from the responsible organs of the United Nations. In the circumstances, he has shown great skill and discretion in handling these problems.

If the Security Council or General Assembly authorizes the Secretary-General to dispatch United Nations forces, it is the responsibility of the Secretary-General to see that the mission is carried out in accordance with the spirit and letter of the resolution. Thereafter, unless he receives specific direction from the Security Council or General Assembly, he must act on his own responsibility. He cannot abdicate his responsibility because of disagreement among the Member States as to how that responsibility can best be exercised. If he did, the office of the Secretary-General would become as impotent as the Military Staff Committee. The Secretary-General rightly took the position in the Congo controversy at the beginning of the Fifteenth Session of the General Assembly that he could not perform his executive functions and maintain the integrity of his office if his right to carry out powers delegated to him could be thwarted, not by the action of a responsible United Nations organ, but by the conflicting views of Member States. It was indeed fortunate that the Secretary-General's interpretation of the constitutional powers of his office received the overwhelming support of the members of the General Assembly.

It is important that the Secretary-General have authority to carry out the responsibilities imposed on his office. It is neither wise nor sound policy, however, for the Security Council or General Assembly to impose excessive responsibilities for basic political decisions on the Secretary-General. In times of emergency or crisis it may be unavoidable. But the authorizing resolution of the Security Council or General Assembly ought to define with as reasonable clarity and specificity as possible the mandate entrusted to the Secretary-General. The recurrent and excessive delegation of policy-making powers to the Secretary-General can impose an unbearable strain upon his office.

Experience both in the Middle East and in the Congo underscores the importance of the Security Council or the General Assembly defining in advance the authority to be exercised by the United Nations Command if United Nations forces are to be employed in specified territories. In the absence of a more definite mandate, the Secretary-General has proceeded on the theory that United Nations forces can enter and operate in the host state only with the consent of the host state. That may be true as a general rule when the forces operate under a resolution of the General Assembly. The situation might be different in the case of Security Council if there is a threat or breach of peace. Although the consent of the host state may be required, experience and sound practice suggest that, so far as practicable, the United Nations organs should make clear to the host state the authority to be assumed and the functions and activities to be performed by the United Nations forces. The host state may then decide whether or not it wishes to accept the United Nations forces on the conditions defined by the United Nations authorities. The host state should not be allowed to manipulate its consent so as to control or obstruct the operations of the United Nations forces. The United Nations must accept the responsibility for determining the conditions under which its forces will operate. The host state may accept or reject these conditions but it should not be accorded the right to dictate the conditions under which the United Nations forces will operate. The more clearly the conditions are defined in advance by the United Nations authorities, the less likelihood there will be of misunderstanding and friction. It is to be regretted that time did not permit a clearer definition of the authority to be assumed by the United Nations forces in the Congo before the dispatch of the forces. Had the Security Council initially defined the authority of the United Nations Command with the same particularity as it did in its February 21, 1961 resolution, it is possible that some of our present difficulties in the Congo could have been averted, although that resolution itself is far from adequate.

Experience both in the Middle East and in the Congo leaves no doubt that United Nations forces are an indispensable instrument in maintaining peace under the Charter. But the same experience indicates the present impracticability of prescribing in advance, by any general rule or formula, the responsibility of Member States for the composition of the needed forces.

It is interesting to contrast the ability of the United Nations organs to obtain, on an *ad hoc* basis, national contingents for a UN force in the Middle East and in the Congo, with the inability of the Security Council to implement Article 43 of the Charter calling for agreements with Member States for the general availability of the Military Staff Committee to function under Article 44. Of course many difficulties concerning the organization, maintenance, and operation of these *ad hoc* forces remain unsolved. A permanent planning unit with military staff officers in the Secretariat is needed. But experience does suggest that efforts to devise arrangements on an *ad hoc* basis hold more promise than any generalized plan not tailored to the occasion. As Justice Holmes would say: "General propositions do not decide concrete cases."[16] The United Nations forces required to meet the needs and interests of the Middle East are not the same forces or contingents as are required to meet the needs and interests of the Congo. At the time of the Korean operation the United States felt that its military burden was not sufficiently shared by other members, but it is doubtful whether any more equitable sharing could have been achieved at the time. At this stage of development it may be more important to utilize the national interests of Member States in behalf of international organization than to rely upon the general interest of Member States in world peace. At the present stage of development it must be recognized that the interests of states, or their consciousness of their interests, in various areas of conflict in the world differ greatly and that

16 *Lockner v. New York,* 198 United States 45, 76 (1905).

such interests cannot be made to respond to any abstract formula.

*　*　*

I have tried in my first two chapters to trace some of the most significant constitutional developments in the United Nations during the first fifteen years of its life. These developments represent less a logical pattern of growth than a struggle for survival. It would be a mistake to pretend that the United Nations has realized the high hopes of its founders. But it has in a divided world torn by revolutionary conflicts survived trials that its founders never dreamed it could survive. In the following chapter I will try to give some thought to what might be done to strengthen the United Nations and humanity's hope for survival.

Chapter 3

"If we could First Know where we are, and whither we are Tending, we could better Judge what to do and how to do it." — Abraham Lincoln.

IN MY FIRST CHAPTER I examined some of the most significant interpretations given to the charter powers of various organs of the United Nations. These interpretations were found to have construed the Charter liberally, as Marshall and Holmes had construed our own Constitution, to enable the political organism which the Founding Fathers had created to weather heavy storms and to meet and survive unforeseen exigencies.

In Chapter 2, I considered the charter responsibilities of Member States, including the prudent exercise of their charter rights and privileges. I examined in particular the charter obligation of Member States to refrain from the threat or use of force in any manner inconsistent with the purposes of the Charter.

WHAT TO DO?

This review of some of the principal constitutional developments in the United Nations during the first fifteen years of its existence significantly reveals the remarkable qualities of survival and adaptability which inhere in the present Charter. While these fifteen years have been a bitter disappointment for those who had hoped for whole-hearted and good-faith cooperation among the Great Powers to make the United Nations work, it is a tribute to the enduring character of the institution which the Charter created that the United Nations as an institution has survived.

We should not, however, let our hopes for the United Nations blind us to hard facts. The United Nations since its beginning has encountered rough weather, and rough weather still lies ahead.

When the Charter was drafted it was hoped that the Great Powers could work out an acceptable peace which the United Nations could maintain. But a stable and acceptable peace—a consensus, or modicum of understanding or agreement, on the basic principles of peaceful coexistence—was never established after the last World War. The absence of a sound or even relatively stable and acceptable peace at the start of the United Nations has made its task immeasurably more difficult than had been anticipated. The very survival of the United Nations under these circumstances attests to humanity's essential need of the United Nations as an instrument of international cooperation in a world which has become increasingly interdependent despite its ideological differences.

When we consider the adequacy of the Charter, its potentialities and its deficiencies, we must be mindful of the very troubled conditions of the world in which we live and in which the United Nations must operate. We must not in our preoccupation with the symptoms of the world difficulties lose sight of the root causes of those difficulties.

Throughout the world in widely different ways and under widely different circumstances men and nations are struggling to adjust themselves to the radically changed conditions of life which modern science and technology are bringing about. A large part of the world is in the thrall of a fanatical totalitarian ideology which accepts as necessary the present sacrifice of individual freedom and dignity for a dictatorially planned development of mass welfare. Another substantial part of the world, although greatly handicapped by hunger, disease, and illiteracy, impatiently aspires, regardless of human costs, to freedom and independence from any vestige of colonial, feudal, or even trusteeship status, as a necessary first step in its emancipation from economic hardship which past generations fatalistically accepted as inevitable. The rest of the world of which we are a part, at widely different stages of economic development and cherishing in widely varying degrees traditional ideals of freedom and individual liberty, is also struggling to provide enlarged opportunities for all of their people to work

66

for and share in the increased well-being which modern science and technology make possible.

In one way or another the whole world is adjusting itself to revolutionary changes, and the adjustment in many areas is difficult, painful, and not altogether rational. While in an armed world, military strength must be maintained to guard against aggression, military strength based on national armaments is at best only a holding operation necessary to give the world time to make the adjustments required to provide that social, economic, and political health for which humanity is striving. Sustained efforts through the United Nations to assist in this peaceful adjustment of the world to the promise of advancing knowledge may in the long run contribute more to the maintenance of peace than defensive military efforts and alliances.

The United Nations did not create these vexing problems which confront the world today. But the United Nations is a living institution representative of the world as it is. If the United Nations did not reflect the trouble, strife, and want of health which exist in the world today, it would indeed be a failure. It would be divorced from the realities of international life. It would be a facade concealing and not revealing the problems of our troubled world. The United Nations is not the cause of the ferment in the world today. There would be greater ferment if there were no United Nations.

Indeed, one of the important functions of the United

Nations is to reflect the turmoil and trouble in the world, to alert us to what is happening in the world, to inform us of the repercussions of, and reactions to, these happenings in other parts of the world, and to give timely warning of approaching storms. I should think that the reports of our experienced diplomatic observers at the United Nations would or could give a better understanding and perspective of what is happening in the world than could be gleaned from the reports of our diplomatic observers in any other of the great capitals of the world.

But the United Nations is not a self-operating mechanism which can automatically maintain and enforce peace. The United Nations can give its members the means and opportunity of informing themselves of the world's problems and difficulties. The United Nations can serve as the instrument through which its members may voluntarily cooperate and, if they will, combine their moral and material strength in support of the purposes and principles of the Charter. The effectiveness of the United Nations, however, depends not only on the lettered provisions of the Charter, but more importantly on the will and determination of the nations of the world to make it work, and upon the wisdom, imagination, and resourcefulness that their statesmen bring to that task.

The United Nations has had a creditable record of achievements from Iran (1945) to Indonesia (1947), to Berlin (1948), to Korea (1950), to Suez (1956).

But its accomplishments have been marred, its work gravely handicapped, and its future existence jeopardized, by the failure of the Great Powers to agree on the terms on which they will cooperate among themselves and with other nations to maintain the peace through the United Nations. This failure of the Great Powers to agree is not merely due to their failure to agree on a voting formula. It is more fundamental. It betokens a lack of a common faith and the absence of a vital consensus.

It is important that we recognize and face boldly the difficulties which confront the United Nations if these difficulties are to be overcome before it is too late. In the words of Justice Brandeis, "If we would guide by the light of reason, we must let our minds be bold."[1]

We may take hope as well as warning from the fact that similar difficulties were encountered under our Constitution before the Civil War. We now tend to forget that there were those who, in the early days of the American Republic, thought the American Union was a failure and a mistake. There was talk of nullification in Virginia and in Kentucky at the time of the Alien and Sedition Acts. There were thoughts of secession in New England at the time of the War of 1812. Later on, when the halls of Congress reverberated in bitter, cold-war debate over the slavery issue, many on both sides did not share Lincoln's faith in the Constitution, but wanted to break up the Union and go their

[1] *Ice Co. v. Liebman,* 285 United States 262, 311 (1932).

69

separate ways. They attributed the difficulties in the way of peaceful settlement of the slavery issue to deficiencies in the Constitution rather than to deficiencies in their own vision, faith, and resourcefulness.

Our task is to find the means to make effective the fundamental law of the Charter. The principal commitments of the Member States under the Charter are, as I have said, two: First, to refrain in their international relations from the threat or use of force except in individual or collective self-defense [Article 2 (4) and Article 51]; and second, to settle their international disputes by peaceful means in such a manner that peace and security and justice are not endangered [Article 2 (3)]. These are clear and unqualified obligations of the Member States. It is time that the Great Powers, the permanent members of the Security Council, review their interest in the United Nations and, in particular, in the observance of these basic commitments.

It may be said that long before the coming of the nuclear age the important powers had overwhelmingly greater common interests in the maintenance of peace than divergent or conflicting interests in the gains of war. The risks of war even then were too great to be rationally accepted, and yet efforts to keep the peace proved unavailing. Before the nuclear age, however, there was neither common knowledge nor common conviction that all-out war would be mutually suicidal and would threaten the survival of civilization on the earth.

Nations are now aware as they have never been before of the dangers of war to their national existence. The instinct of survival becomes, as it has never been before, a new force uniting mankind in the struggle for peace. Even the most fanatical faiths and ideologies balk at self-destruction. Even the most realistic statesmen have become aware that there are no returns from all-out nuclear war. Man's greatest fear, war's threat to man's survival, may paradoxically become man's greatest hope in the struggle for peace.

Antagonistic ideologies not reconcilable by logic have in the past been reconciled by the felt necessities of the times, even when they contended not only for the things of this earth but for man's immortal soul. Slowly and surely the most hard-headed statesmen— even the leaders and dictators of totalitarian governments—are coming to realize that war no longer is a practical way of adjusting international disputes or differences.

If nuclear war is to be eliminated, all war must be eliminated as a means of adjusting disputes between nations. For once the killing starts, unless promptly stopped, there can be no assurance that it can be contained or limited either to specified areas or specified weapons. When nations fight to kill they are not likely to be particular about the manner or place of killing. In this nuclear age war must be banished if civilization as we have known it is to survive.

Until we achieve general disarmament we should have a balanced and flexible defense, including con-

71

ventional arms to deter limited wars and adventurism and to oppose armed coups while efforts are being made to stop the fighting. But the Charter does not permit, and wise statesmanship should never sanction, the acceptance of war of any kind, limited or unlimited, as an instrument of national policy.

We must therefore strengthen the consensus among all nations, and among the Great Powers in particular, that force must not be used as an arbiter of international differences. A consensus, a common conviction, a consciously shared interest, can produce a workable voting formula or operate under various voting formulae. But a voting formula cannot produce a consensus of mind or feeling. The problem of consensus is encountered in national as well as international affairs. Even in the United States, where there is a general consensus that we should abide by the rule of the majority subject only to the Constitution, we encounter great difficulties when our people are bitterly divided on geographic lines as they have been in the area of civil rights. Similarly, France has suffered acutely from her inability up until now to develop a sufficiently strong and broad consensus to deal with her Algerian problem.

Consensus involves a sense of sharing and participating quite as much as a sense of agreement. Men are more willing to accept a law or ruling with which they disagree if they feel that the law or ruling comes from a community of which they are a part, represents the general sentiments and feelings of the community as a whole, and is not imposed by one section of the community upon another. If we wish to develop, strengthen, and build upon a consensus in the United Nations we must develop a community feeling, a shared feeling that not one state or group of states is imposing its will on another state or group of states, but that the community of nations is acting in the common interest of all members to reduce and eliminate the danger of war.[2] We must rely more upon an appeal to reason and common interest and less upon the power to vote.

Because communist ideology scorns bourgeois thinking, we seem ourselves to have lost faith in the power of right reason to penetrate the communist curtain, even in an appeal to communist self-interest. We seem to have lost Jefferson's faith in the power of reason if free to combat error, to triumph over it. The West and the Soviet Union each acts as if the only language the other could understand is the language of force.

Patterns of the past rise to haunt us. Were we not told at the height of the Nazi menace that we cannot reason with a rattlesnake? But that was said when a limited European war was already bursting its limits. Let us not forget that when reason might still have penetrated the Nazi curtain we were busy passing

[2] See Lincoln P. Bloomfield, "The United States, the United Nations and the Creation of Community," *International Organization* 14: 503 (1960).

neutrality legislation vainly trying to isolate ourselves from the world.

It is not suggested that we relax our vigilance, or unilaterally reduce our armaments, or lessen our attachment to human freedom and dignity, or condone any wrong or injustice. It is suggested, however, that the arms race and the Cold War if continued are likely to increase the danger of suicidal war. The Cold War has hardened and sharpened the differences between the West and the Soviet Union. It has not helped to resolve or contain them.

Harrison Brown and James Real have written a moving pamphlet on the *Community of Fear,*[3] describing the nature of the arms race, the terrifying dimensions of destruction that nuclear weapons have reached, and the even more terrifying dimensions of destruction they will reach if the arms race continues. It is written so that if read by a citizen of the West or by a Soviet citizen, either of them must become poignantly aware of mankind's common interest in avoiding a nuclear holocaust and the need of a fresh approach if we are to avoid it. As Dr. Reinhold Niebuhr observes in the Foreword:

"This study, for the first time I think, gives vivid images of the terrifying possibilities in the thermonuclear weapons, and of the annihilation of space and time which is the consequence of technical advances in the delivery system. This latter development makes

[3] Published by The Fund for the Republic, September 1960.

war by miscalculation or misadventure more and more a probability rather than a possibility. * * * Ultimately the ever-accelerated pace of the arms race must lead to disaster even if neither side consciously desires the ultimate war. * * * A fresh approach is needed, prompted by the awareness of the common danger, rather than by the complacent assumption of either side that they are strong enough to prevent an attack or win the war if it should come. * * * * I will merely observe that such an approach must obviously begin at the only place where a sense of community has been established, across the chasm of a great ideological and power conflict. That minimal community has been established through the sense of an involvement in a common predicament and peril."

We must make that sense of community of interest in the maintenance of peace of which Dr. Niebuhr speaks the motivating force of the United Nations. It is time that the Great Powers should say to one another in the words of Isaiah: "Come now and let us reason together." Let us consider what we can do to protect our common interest in the maintenance of peace. But we must not expect miracles to happen overnight. It will not be easy to change the patterns of thought which have dominated both sides during the period of the Cold War. It will take time to dispel deeply rooted suspicions and doubts. Reason can identify but not resolve many strongly felt differences in ideas and values.

The recognition of the community of interest in peace does not mean that differences in vital interests and ideological commitments will cease to exist between nations. But if the recognition and consciousness of the common interest in peace of all nations, and of the Great Powers in particular, are strong enough, we might venture to hope that nations would strive to narrow and contain, if not to settle, those differences and make a genuine effort to avoid the exploitation and sharpening of those differences. Up to the present time, however, there has been inadequate effort on the part of the Great Powers to narrow and contain disputes which could precipitate conflict and war to the mutual and irreparable harm of all concerned.

The leaders of the Great Powers that have the greatest stakes in the maintenance of peace should recognize that they have a common problem and face a common dilemma. That is, how to prevent disputes between them, which involve their vital interests, from embroiling them in armed conflict much more disastrous to their vital interests than any disposition of these disputes short of war could possibly be.

If the Great Powers could concentrate on this one common problem and dilemma, in which their interests are and must be common, isolating it for the time being from the discussion of particular quarrels and differences where their interests diverge, perhaps some new and constructive approaches to a consensus could be found. It is certainly time that the leaders of civilized nations should begin talking sense to one another with a view to finding a solution to this common problem and dilemma upon whose solution the very survival of civilized mankind would seem to depend. We should take the initiative in talking reason and sense to the Russians, despite repeated rebuffs, until they do hear and understand. Too often the communications between the West and the Soviet Union are self-serving and self-justifying propaganda intended to please the home folk but not calculated to convince the other side. Even with the establishment of serious and meaningful communication between the Great Powers, there would be no pat or easy solution to the dilemma. But if the problem were approached as a common task for joint exploration, new and promising approaches to the problem might open up.

I am neither forgetting Red China nor excluding her from participation in this joint exploration. It may take time for her revolutionary and ideological fervor, which has been fanned by her isolation, to cool. But it is well to remember that at the end of the second World War when our planes were being shot down on the border of Yugoslavia it seemed more difficult to talk to Tito than to Stalin. China also has an interest in mankind's survival and sooner or later will become conscious of that interest.

It would certainly give a great lift to the United Nations and the prospect for world peace if the Great Powers, the permanent members of the Security Council, were to announce that they planned to hold within the framework of the United Nations a series of high-level conferences with a view to developing a consensus on certain over-all approaches to reduce or contain within tolerable limits international tensions and differences. It would then be understood that if and when a consensus was reached on given approaches, these would be pursued on a continuing basis in collaboration with other members.

There has been much debate on the value of high-level conferences, and I do not wish to become involved in a prolonged discussion of their uses, abuses, and dangers. But it is not an accident that heads of states and foreign secretaries find it impossible to avoid such conferences. With delegations in constant and instantaneous communication with their home offices, there are in a sense today no plenipotentiaries. The really important decisions involving basic policy are and can be made only at the highest level. With the growing complexities of foreign affairs, even the best-run foreign offices are unable to avoid bureaucratic rigidities, and only the highest officials feel free, or at least are believed to be free, to consider changes in established policies and procedures. It is not the simplest thing in the world for even the head of a modern state to overturn established policies and procedures. It is true that conferences at a very high level lack the continuity necessary to resolve matters requiring protracted negotiations. But, if properly prepared through diplomatic channels and if not overdramatized for propaganda purposes, high-level conferences can be of great value in revitalizing contacts at other levels, in setting new directions, and in breaking through log-jams and roadblocks. Instead of taking a completely negative or unnecessarily defensive attitude towards high-level conferences, we should not only let our people understand their limitations, but appreciate their need and value.

It is important that the suggested conferences be held at the United Nations as a reminder to the Great Powers that they are not acting for themselves alone but are preparing a broadened consensus for the whole community of Member States. Such conferences should be convened at the United Nations as an assurance to the smaller powers that their interests in the peace will not be neglected and that at an appropriate time they will be consulted and brought into the consensus. Such conferences should also be at the United Nations to give emphasis to the fact that they are not to be a dramatic one-shot affair but the beginning of a continuing quest for peace to be pursued at all levels.

What are some of the fields that the Great Powers could select for joint exploration to strengthen and maintain the consensus that world peace must be preserved and war avoided?

1) First of all, there is urgent need of renewed and determined collaboration to stop the arms race before it drives the human race underground. As a beginning,

79

there should be a renewed effort to reach agreement on the cessation of nuclear testing under appropriate inspection and control. The negotiators should be instructed to try to understand each other's difficulties and find ways of meeting those difficulties without impairing the objectives or effectiveness of the agreement. Such a nuclear test-suspension agreement is a small start in itself, but its significance as a genuine start in the right direction is very great. It would reduce the hazards to health of fall-outs from atmospheric tests. It would slow down the arms race, and it is necessary to slow down the arms race before any agreed cut-back in arms can have any real significance. It will not help to cut back on less important and obsolescent arms if we continue to race to make better and more deadly arms. The test suspension would provide an experiment in international inspection on a limited scale which would be of great value in devising inspection plans for other arms control measures. It would bring the East and the West together in technical tasks of arms control which will enable them better to appreciate the reality of their common interest in the maintenance of peace. To secure the agreement of some of the more important non-nuclear powers to stop testing, further concessions in the way of the control of existing stockpiles will probably be required. This should encourage the Russians as well as ourselves to work together on more comprehensive measures of arms control to prevent the spread of nuclear weapons to other countries.

Following or accompanying a test-cessation agreement, I should hope that a special collaborative effort
would be made to secure by monitored agreements
openness and full disclosure of all activities, whether
by way of missiles or satellites, that involve a penetra-
tion of outer-space. The great Danish scientist, Niels
Bohr, has stressed the importance of openness and the
lifting of secrecy as an essential prerequisite to progress
in the field of arms control.[4] Secrecy is such an old and
ingrained habit that it is difficult to accustom ourselves
to the disclosure of all of our secrets and to living in
the light. If we cannot as yet secure a completely open
world, perhaps we can secure openness in outer-space.
To acquire openness in all ventures into outer-space
before nations acquire vested interests in the secrets of
outer-space would seem practicable. It should be possible to establish a monitoring system to detect the
sending of any missiles or satellites into outer-space. It
should therefore be feasible to require notification and
disclosure of all activities in outer-space. There should
be no secrets of any kind in such ventures. This would
not suppress the scientist's quest for knowledge but it
would lessen the fear of one side or the other's scoring
a scientific break-through which would destroy the
existing uneasy balance of power and endanger the
peace. It would bring the scientists of the West and the
East together in common tasks of inspection and monitoring and would open the way for their cooperation

[4] See Niels Bohr, "For an Open World," *Bulletin of Atomic Scientists*, 6: 213 (July 1950).

81

in exploratory ventures in outer-space. The more citizens of the East and citizens of the West can work together at all levels of contact, governmental and non-governmental, on tasks where their interests and purposes are common and not divergent, the more they are likely to develop the will to reconcile or at least live with their differences. Common ventures into outer-space, common scientific explorations, common health programs, all of these can help give reality to our common interest in our common peace.

2) In the second place, there is real room and need for joint exploration by the West and the Soviet Union to discover and maintain the essential rules and conditions of peaceful coexistence.

Despite our faltering efforts in the field of disarmament we have succeeded in linking disarmament and arms limitations with inspection and control, and in convincing world opinion that one cannot be had without the other. Similarly, instead of taking a negative attitude towards the Russian plea for peaceful coexistence, we must convince the Russians and world opinion that, if peaceful coexistence is to have meaning, there must be agreement on the minimum essential conditions or rules of peaceful coexistence. We should at all times link the idea of peaceful coexistence with the rules necessary to make such coexistence possible. There must be some consensus not only on the objectives of peaceful coexistence but some consensus on the rules of peaceful coexistence. Sober study and serious exchange of ideas will be necessary to determine the nature and scope of the rules essential for peaceful co-existence. Such rules must be equally binding on, and respected by, all concerned. We will succeed in agreeing upon such rules only if both the West and the Soviet Union are convinced that agreement on such rules is necessary to protect their common interest in the maintenance of peace.

In this connection I do not have in mind any general codification of the rules of international law. We are passing through a period when even the old rules of international law, inadequate as they were to prevent armed strife between states, have been greatly eroded by disregard and disuse. The new ground rules for peaceful coexistence, if they are to have vitality, must have regard for the political needs of the present as much as or even more than the legal traditions of the past.

It will serve little purpose to engage in recriminations as to who is responsible for the erosion of international law in the world today. Certainly the non-communist world cannot today rely upon the communist states' observing the traditional rules of law when it does not suit their purposes. Their false charges of germ warfare in Korea is evidence of how far they have gone in misusing international law for ulterior purposes. Non-communist states may well object to the communist states' rejecting international law in some areas and then expecting its observance by

83

non-communist states in other areas. But we should not deceive ourselves as to the extent that the communist attitude towards international law has affected our own action. Unfortunately, Gresham's Law is operative in the field of international law and diplomacy. One need only refer to the U-2 incident,[5] and should also recall the recent incident in which a prominent member of the Foreign Relations Committee called upon the State Department to protest the Soviet Union's conducting missile tests that would interfere with free navigation on the high seas, forgetting that we had been conducting such tests for years.

While communism as a revolutionary force may reject bourgeois law, the Soviet as an established state in this nuclear age has a vital interest in the maintenance of peace, and peace cannot be made secure without some accepted rules of international conduct. Without engaging in a dialectic controversy as to the effectiveness and enforceability of the whole body of international law, it should be in the interest of the principal non-communist and communist nations to attempt to reach some consensus as to the rules of international conduct to be observed in the most sensitive areas of their relationships so as to reduce the danger of war.[6]

One such sensitive area would be the trade and commercial relations between the West and the Soviet

---

[5] Quincy Wright, "Legal Aspects of the U-2 Incident," *American Journal of International Law,* 54: 836 (1960).

[6] See John N. Hazard, "Codifying Peaceful Coexistence," *American Journal of International Law,* 55: 109 (January 1961).

Union. Trade can be used not only to improve relations between states, but to increase and aggravate tensions. If peaceful coexistence is to embrace peaceful trade and commerce between states with different social and economic systems, there must be rules not only to encourage trade on the basis of comparative advantage but to afford some protection against trade being used for purposes of economic warfare and the Cold War.[7]

Another most sensitive area where the absence of ground rules involves grave danger to the maintenance of peace concerns the relations of established states to the underdeveloped states and to the power-vacuum or so-called "gray" areas of the world. Unless the Great Powers are able to agree on ground rules to facilitate the orderly development of these areas, to control the shipment of arms to such areas, and to prevent them from being used as pawns in a struggle for power between rival systems, there is danger of real trouble which could precipitate a chain reaction culminating in war before the people who must pay the price know what has happened. As Professor Quincy Wright points out, the existing law on subversive intervention is far from clear.[8] Whatever be the law, too little respect for

[7] See Berman, Lipson, and Shapiro, "Soviet Law and East-West Trade," *The Record of the Association of the Bar of the City of New York*, 16: 26 (January 1961); Raymond Vernon, "A Trade Policy for the 1960's," *Foreign Affairs*, 39: 458, 467 (April 1961).

[8] "Subversive Intervention," *American Journal of International Law*, 54: 521 (July 1960).

it is shown by either the communist or the non-communist states. When fighting breaks out in Laos, how many people really know what is going on behind the scenes—to what extent the Great Powers may become involved in war because of adventurism on one or both sides?

Present difficulties in the Congo only foreshadow the problems which will beset the relations between the communist and non-communist states in their contacts with the newly emerging African states. Despite the differences between the Great Powers, they all have much more to gain from peaceful co-operation than from imperial or ideological rivalry which could lead first to armed conflict among the Africans and then to world war, perhaps to world end.

Indeed, the rivalry between the West and the Soviet Union for position and influence with the new states just emerging from colonial status may result in both sides' neglecting to protect their common interest in the peaceful and orderly developments of these new states. The new states not only cherish their independence but expect to share in the revolution of rising expectations. But in this interdependent world there can be no revolution of rising expectations in underdeveloped lands without access to the tools and know-how of modern science and technology. If colonialism is succeeded not by enlightened international co-operation but by narrow isolationism or resurgent tribalism, political and economic conditions in the new

86

states are likely to deteriorate dangerously. If that happens in this increasingly interdependent world, East and West and North and South will suffer. We in the West should not forget the price our generation has had to pay for a past generation's indifference to Russia's and China's failure to participate adequately in the industrial progress of the nineteenth century.

The Soviet Union and the West have been so embroiled in the Cold War that they both have tended to view Asia and Africa, and even South America, as mere battlefields in that Cold War. We should wake up to the facts of life: Asia and Africa and South America are the homes of free and independent nations which will increasingly expect to be treated as such. We should not repeat the mistakes of nineteenth-century imperialism. It is high time that we of the West and the Soviet Union realize how important it is to both of us to have a peaceful world to live in. We are not going to have such a world unless we can work out the essential rules and conditions of peaceful coexistence satisfactory not only to ourselves but to the world-wide membership of the United Nations.

3) But even if the West and the Soviet Union can succeed in putting some brakes on the arms race and in spelling out a few ground rules for peaceful coexistence, that will be only a beginning. In this deeply divided world there will remain many serious conflicts of interest and disputes of major proportions between the non-communist West and the Communist East.

87

A third field, therefore, which deserves common exploration by the Great Powers is the treatment and handling of disputes on which the Great Powers remain in profound and, for the time being, irreconcilable disagreement.

Some might suggest that there is one, simple answer to this problem and that is to agree to the settlement of these disputes by the rule of law. The difficulty is, as has already been observed, that the applicable international law is fragmentary, shadowy, and often nonexistent. The issues involved are generally not strictly legal, but political, and often relate to the problem of peaceful change for which the law provides no adequate or quick solution. But that does not mean where strictly legal issues are involved we should not press for their submission to judicial disposition. Certainly the time has come for the United States to withdraw its self-judging reservation to its acceptance of the compulsory jurisdiction of the International Court of Justice.

There is, however, no easy way of settling the political disputes concerning which the Great Powers are bitterly divided. It should not be impossible, however, if the Great Powers truly regard the avoidance of war as their paramount interest, for them to develop a consensus as to the ground rules to be observed to prevent such disputes from erupting into war. Instead of exploiting such disputes for propaganda purposes, the Great Powers might agree to seek to narrow their differences and not deliberately keep open irritating

88

minor differences susceptible of settlement without a surrender of principle. They might also agree to seek to devise provisional arrangements which would contain their disputes within tolerable limits and allow time to provide a solvent for problems for which no agreed solution is presently possible. They might agree not to agitate for the settlement of issues which they know cannot presently be settled when they know the agitation cannot help but only inflame the situation. It is significant that Ambassador Lodge, having himself entered the United Nations as a Cold War warrior, should have remarked, on leaving, that we must win the Cold War by ending it.

Possibly all effort to reach a working consensus on the matters I have discussed will fail. But I for one am unwilling to abandon hope in reason. These are matters in which we have a common interest to find agreement. We should not be discouraged if our appeals to reason do not evoke immediate response. It takes time as well as reason to reach minds that are deeply suspicious and distrustful. It takes time for bureaucratic and ideological ideas to change. It is important that we judge the effectiveness of our action not by the immediate response or tomorrow's press headlines but by Russia's or China's action two, five, and even ten years hence.

In this nuclear age we must put our faith in time as the great solvent of our difficulties. We must put our faith in time to give right reason its chance to win

89

its way. Mr. Krushchev says time is on the communist side without resort to force. The West should be willing to accept that challenge and accept time as the arbiter with resort to force ruled out. If the West is true to its own traditions it will put its confidence in the power of its ideas of freedom, justice, and human welfare to prevail in a world free from the fear of war.

We must seek through a developing consensus not only to arrest and reverse the arms race but to arrest and reverse the Cold War. True competition in the international field consists not in defaming and degrading nor in embarrassing and enraging your competitor but in producing proof of the ability of your way of life to excel that of your competitor in satisfying human needs and aspirations. As a discerning British scientist has recently said, "It is not the political system which can put the biggest satellite in orbit which will win lasting honor, but that which will provide the greatest increase in human welfare."[9]

The Cold War has obscured rather than illuminated the West's attachment to human freedom and well-being. It is difficult particularly for Americans to realize that in many parts of the world there is the feeling that the West is primarily interested in saving freedom and well-being from communism, but that the West does not have the same interest in protecting human freedom and well-being from attacks from other

[9] P. M. S. Blackett, "New Science or Old Technology," *Bulletin of Atomic Scientists*, 17: 53 (February 1961).

sources. It is difficult to deny that if the United States had been equally concerned in the last decade with the threat of any and all forms of tyranny and dictatorship in the Western Hemisphere, there would be less ground for concern today about the threat of a communist dictatorship in Cuba.

If the Great Powers want to protect their common interest in the maintenance of peace and to make the United Nations work—and the two objectives are really one and inseparable—they must agree before it is too late on the basic ground rules of peaceful and competitive coexistence. Paradoxically this means, as I have suggested, not to settle but to contain their irreconcilable differences which time alone can peacefully resolve. Some may ask whether this is not accepting the *status quo* and perpetuating injustice? The answer is that in the long run justice and fair play will fare better in a friendly, peaceful world than in a world that allows war rather than time to settle our destiny.

Justice Holmes has reminded us that "time has upset many fighting faiths."[10] Time may bring unexpected changes. We should ponder, even though we may not agree with, Nehru's recent remark that the United States and the Soviet Union are more alike than any two countries in the world, and would become even more similar in the future. It is also well to remember that our chief enemies in the last world war —Germany and Japan—are now our allies. That does

[10] *Abrams v. United States*, 250 United States 616, 630 (1918).

91

not mean that we must not be on our guard against giving our trust improvidently and prematurely. But it does mean that we should have patience and perspective.

* * *

If the Great Powers can move to a consensus on the ground rules which they will observe in the United Nations, and encourage the acceptance and observance of similar ground rules by the other members, the usefulness and effectiveness of the United Nations would be enormously increased without any structural changes. Heretofore the United Nations has demonstrated its capacity as an organism to adjust to unexpected exigencies and still survive. With a better consensus on the ground rules the United Nations may be expected to demonstrate its capacity for healthy growth, in ways and in forms that contemporary statesmanship cannot foresee and dare not predict.

In the early days of the Charter, when nothing was more important to the life of the Charter than the rejection of the notion that the Charter was finished if the Great Powers did not work together in the Security Council, it was necessary to stress the authority of the General Assembly to act when the Security Council was unable to act. This led, as has already been indicated, to excessive emphasis on voting and a misguided attempt to exaggerate the significance of a numerical majority. Apart from matters of internal management where voting is necessary, a vote is important if states having power to act are prepared to take collective measures to give effect to the vote, as in the case of Korea. A vote is also important if it represents an overwhelming world-wide response or reaction to events that is reasonably likely to influence the action of the state to which the resolution voted is addressed, if not at once, within a reasonable period of time. But many votes may only serve to strengthen divisions rather than to develop a consensus.

It should be remembered that action of the General Assembly is recommendatory and not mandatory. Its effectiveness must depend upon the strength of its appeal to the judgment and interests of states. Member States may be expected to give good-faith consideration to the recommendations of the General Assembly but they are not bound to act against their better judgment. Nor can a democratic state in fact pursue with vigor a policy opposed by its own people. It must be recognized that voting in the Assembly on the basis of the sovereign equality of states, does not automatically reflect world power, world wealth, world population, or world wisdom. With the admission of many new and relatively weak states, theoretically it becomes possible for the General Assembly to vote for action for the carrying-out of which the voting majority will in fact shoulder little or no responsibility. Small states cannot expect to dictate to the more powerful states what they must do. On the other hand small states also have their rights, and large states cannot claim the right to act in areas in which the small states are concerned without explaining and justifying their action. As President Roosevelt stated in his last State of the Union Message on January 6, 1945. "We cannot deny that power is a factor in world politics any more than we can deny that power is a factor in national politics. But in a democratic world, as in a democratic nation, power must be linked with responsibility and obliged to defend and justify itself within the framework of the general good."

Small and relatively weak states may influence the action of the more powerful states, but they cannot use their voting strength in the General Assembly to dictate. The irresponsible exercise of voting power by the small and relatively weak states may threaten the future of the United Nations quite as much as the irresponsible exercise of the veto or the irresponsible withholding of contributions by the Great Powers. The situation is all the more dangerous because the attitude of many of the new members is deeply affected by their past colonial experience which at times causes them to be deeply suspicious and to react with more bitterness than reason against their former colonial masters. One can only hope that the deeply-felt loyalties of the new members to the United Nations will keep this attitude from getting out of hand. For the present the new members have stood staunchly against the determined efforts of the Soviet Union to weaken and render impotent the United Nations. But should the Soviet Union find ways of exploiting the new members' suspicions of their former colonial masters in order to weaken and make unworkable the office of the Secretary-General and the adminstrative machinery of the United Nations, the United Nations would be in real trouble if not mortal danger.

The General Assembly and the Security Council are both political bodies. As in all political bodies, the delegates often speak more to their own constituents than to their fellow delegates. To some extent, as we have observed, this is unavoidable and within limits desirable. It does in a way enable the delegates to inform and advise one another of the grievances, the problems, and the predilections of their various constituencies. But the Cold War has unfortunately invaded the United Nations and taken over to the point that it strengthens and accentuates divisions and militates against the development of a consensus, against the development of a feeling of community in meeting the problems and adjusting the differences which confront the General Assembly and the Security Council.

If the political organs of the United Nations are to play an important part in building an endurable peace, there must be, when there is no clear consensus, a downgrading of voting, an avoidance of broad moralistic judgments, and an upgrading of efforts to bridge and narrow differences, to mediate and conciliate, to seek accommodations and compromises, and leave to

95

the solvent of time and unforeseeable events the solution of seemingly irreconcilable conflicts.

Efforts to mediate peaceful settlements and to find practical accommodations may in themselves help us to find new means of achieving a consensus and even to develop working rules of law. Let us remember that the fruitful periods of legal codification have occurred after and not during periods of legal growth. Let us seek practical settlements based upon mutual tolerance so that future generations may survive to reach a consensus which our generation is unable to reach.

Blind groping for practical settlement with no principles to guide us, except those shadowy ones found within the vague contours of the Charter, may not appeal to lawyers who take their jurisprudence from Austin. But such procedures do not differ radically from those we employ in the domestic field to settle labor disputes. As the Charter forbids resort to force, so we deny the use of force in labor disputes. As the Charter imposes the duty to settle disputes peacefully, so management and labor are duty-bound to settle their disputes by peaceful means. Particular means are not prescribed but some means must be found, and all means cannot be rejected. Of course it is an imperfect system, a transitional system, a system which must be made to work until a better consensus is developed and accepted.

In this period when international law is experiencing growing pains there is conflict between the lawyers and the diplomats as to the role of law in diplomacy and the role of diplomacy in law. Some lawyers would like to feel that the progressive development of international law was almost their exclusive province. Some students of diplomacy have deprecated the activities of lawyers in the field of diplomacy and would even cast doubt on their qualifications to hold diplomatic or high-level foreign policy positions. Some lawyers may make poor diplomats and some diplomats may have little to contribute to the progressive development of the law. If at times an excessively legalistic or moralistic attitude creeps into our diplomacy it is as often as not traceable to others than lawyers, certainly not to "good lawyers." In this period of transition and growth a rigid separation of law and diplomacy is neither desirable nor possible, and a cross-fertilization of the two disciplines can contribute much.

* * *

In emphasizing the potentialities of organic and constitutional growth under the Charter, I do not wish to rule out all Charter amendments. I only warn that we must exploit the potentialities of the present Charter in order to develop a broader consensus and a deeper feeling of world-wide community which must precede any meaningful Charter change. As we broaden the areas of consensus we increase the possibility of strengthening the Charter by amendment. But

97

without a broadened consensus we are neither likely to be able to strengthen the Charter through amendment nor to find amendments workable or effective if by accident they were obtained.

There does seem to be developing a consensus that the Security Council should be enlarged to be more representative of the enlarged United Nations membership. But when the Security Council is enlarged I should hope that not only would additional representation be accorded the new and smaller states but that additional representation should be accorded the middle states by creating additional permanent members without power of veto, or at least an additional class of members eligible for re-election. This middle group should include states like India, Japan, Brazil, Italy and, if and when united, Germany and possibly Nigeria. If there is no agreement on an enlarged Security Council I should expect in time to see the General Assembly remain more or less continuously in session and a broadly representative standing committee of the General Assembly established which would come more and more to perform the role intended for the Security Council.

In light of the great disparity in power between the small number of large states and the large number of small states, the question of weighted voting in the General Assembly recurrently arises. It is not easy to find any acceptable principle of weighted voting to impose on the principle of the sovereign equality of states. Most proposals for weighted voting raise as many difficulties as they solve. Some proposals would only give added significance to voting with no assurance that the voting would reflect a broader or better consensus. Nevertheless on the financial side, particularly in the administration of special funds, it is possible that voting formulas similar to those employed in the Monetary Fund and World Bank could be advantageously employed. It might also be conceivably possible, if and when the Great Powers consent to the enlargement of the Security Council in order to have a more balanced representation, that the smaller states might consent to a requirement that ordinary resolutions of the General Assembly should be passed by a double majority vote—that is, by a majority of all members of the United Nations and by a majority of the states represented on the enlarged Security Council. Then important resolutions of the General Assembly would require a two-thirds majority of the whole membership and a similar majority of the states on the Security Council.[11] This is a form of weighted voting which avoids the need for weighting the votes of the individual states.

* * *

It may possibly be thought that I have dwelt too much on the need of developing a consensus to reduce

[11] See 13th Report, Commission to Study the Organization of Peace (January, 1961), p. 39.

the friction between the communist and non-communist states. It may be urged that the real challenge to the United Nations will come from the newly emergent states in Asia and Africa, and that the difficulties in the Congo are only a foretaste of what will be the regular fare of the United Nations in the future. In a sense this may be true. But if it be true, it is all the more important that we seek to abate the perennial and festering conflict between the Soviet Union and the United States which obstructs the co-operation and blocks the consensus necessary in the United Nations to enable it to meet its affirmative tasks.

Back of our ideological conflict with the Soviet Union, back of the forces impelling the newly emergent states to cast off the yoke of colonialism and feudalism, back of the movement for New Deals and New Freedoms in the West, is a common revolutionary force. Properly understood, it should unite and not divide mankind. It should unite mankind in a common co-operative effort to secure the new freedoms and the new well-being that progress in science and technology can bring to all mankind if mankind can organize itself to make effective use of this new knowledge. The revolutionary changes which science and technology have set in motion not only are eliminating caste and class within national boundaries but they are eliminating national boundaries as the normal limits of economic and political co-operation. History may record that the basic difference between the United States and the Soviet Union in the second half of the twentieth century was in their conception of the type and degree of economic and political organization required to achieve the increased well-being that science and technology made possible. History may conclude that the United States underestimated—in theory more than in practice—the degree of national and international planning necessary to keep its increasingly interdependent economic system functioning smoothly and with a maximum freedom, while the Soviet Union so grossly overestimated the degree of planning appropriate to give its people the maximum benefits of the new technology that it thought totalitarian controls were necessary for this purpose. History, I fear, may also record that the greatest mistake both powers made was to minimize their common interest in working together to assist in the orderly development of the newly emergent states in Asia and Africa, striving within a few generations to advance from static feudalism and tribalism to modern industrial democracy.

But the more affirmative the tasks of the United Nations may be, the greater the need for developing a consensus of thinking that will make active co-operation possible and meaningful. In this quest for consensus there is no role for dogmatism and self-righteousness. I would close no doors. In the United Nations, as "in my Father's house," there "are many mansions".

Index

INDEX

Dumbarton Oaks Conference, 10

Egypt, 43, 44. *See also* Suez, invasion of

Eisenhower, President Dwight D., 45, 49, 50

Force, use of: Charter provisions on, 3–4, 38, 39–43, 54; in Suez invasion, 43–45, 46, 70; consensus against, 72

Formosa, 28, 46, 47, 48–56

Four Power Statement, 11–14

France: and invasion of Suez, 43–45, 46; and Algeria, 72

Germany, 91, 98. *See also* Berlin

Great Britain: and invasion of Suez, 43–45, 46

Great Powers, role in United Nations, 14, 15; defensive arrangements, 36; stake in peace, 76; disputes between, 77, 88–89; and underdeveloped countries, 85

Guatemala, 42

Hammarskjold, Dag, 58; and Congo crisis, 59. *See also* Secretary-General, the

Holmes, Justice Oliver Wendell, 1, 5, 62, 64, 91

Human rights, 21

India, 98

Indo-China, 26, 35

Indonesia, 35, 68

Inspection: as experiment in arms control, 80–82; in outer-space exploration, 81

International Court of Justice, the, 22; and the United States, 88

International law, 96–97; communist attitudes toward, 83–84; and U-2 incident, 84

Intervention, 23–24, 25, 85–86

Iran, 10, 68

Israel, role in Suez invasion, 43–45

Italian Peace Treaty, 27–28

Italy, 98; and Trieste settlement, 27–28

Japan, 47, 48, 49, 91, 98

Japanese Peace Treaty, 28, 47, 48

Jefferson, Thomas, 73

Katz, Milton, quoted, 39–40, 41

Korean War, 10, 17–18, 28, 48, 62, 68, 83, 92

Krushchev, Nikita, 89

Laos, 35, 42, 56–57, 85

Lauterpacht, H., quoted, 22–23, 24

Lawyers, as diplomats, 97

Lebanon, 42

Lincoln, Abraham, 64, 69

Lodge, Henry Cabot, 89

MacArthur, General Douglas, 47

Marshall, Chief Justice John, 5, 6, 15, 64

Matsu, Island of, 49, 55

McCulloch v. Maryland, 5–6, 18

Middle East, U. N. force in, 60, 61, 62

Military Staff Committee, 59, 62

Missouri v. Holland, 5–6

Mutual Defense Treaty of 1954, 50–51

NATO, 26, 36, 37

Nazis, the, 73

Nehru, Jawaharlal, 91

New states, 66, 85–87, 94–95, 98, 100–101

Niebuhr, Reinhold, quoted, 74–75

Nigeria, 98

Nuclear tests, suspension, 80–81

Nuclear weapons, potentials, 74

INDEX

United Nations: neglect of its pacific functions 35–36, 69; role in world revolution, 67–68; consensus on ground rules, 92; and the Cold War, 35–36; and the emerging nations, 100

United Nations forces, 36, 45; use in Middle East and Congo, 58, 62; conditions for use, 60–61; *ad hoc* forces, 61–62

United Nations organs: competence under Charter, 1–30; role in disarmament, 29; by-passing mediatory functions of, 35, 36; and threats to peace, 42–43; their responsibility for U. N. forces, 60

United States, as Sponsoring Power, 11; and Aswan Dam project, 44; and the Republic of China, 54–55; and International Court of Justice, 88; and Western Hemisphere, 91; and the Soviet Union, 100–101

Uniting for Peace Resolution of 1950, 17–18

Veto power: Austin quoted on, 16; in disarmament agreements, 29. *See also* Double veto

Voting, abstention from, 7–10; significance of, 92; by small states, 94. *See also* Weighted voting

War, 70–72; consensus against, 73

Weighted voting, 98–99

West, the: and the Soviet Union, 73, 74, 77, 84, 86

Wright, Quincy, quoted, 53–54, 85

Yugoslavia, 77; and Trieste settlement, 28

106